MW01137272

THREE
SISTERS

A True Holocaust Story of Love, Luck, and Survival

Memoirs written by

Eva Heymann, Judith Kashti, and Alexandra Littauer

Edited and narrated by Celia Clement

THREE SISTERS
A True Holocaust Story of Love, Luck, and Survival

Memoirs written by
Eva Heymann, Judith Kashti, and Alexandra Littauer

Edited and narrated by Celia Clement

Front cover: Chaville, France, 1939
Left to right bottom row: Judith, Grofa, and Alexandra
Second row: Eva, Fritz, and Lore; Peter in far back (digitally added)

Visit:
www.celia-clement.com

Contact:
celia.threesisters@gmail.com

This book is dedicated to

✑ **Félix Goldschmidt** ❧

who rescued the Kroch family numerous times,
risking his life and placing his family in jeopardy.
He was a hero of the French resistance
who saved not only our family
but several hundred other Jews as well, and continued
his work on behalf of humanity for the rest of his life.
Accounts of his heroism and altruism
are brought to life in this book.

Kroch Family Tree

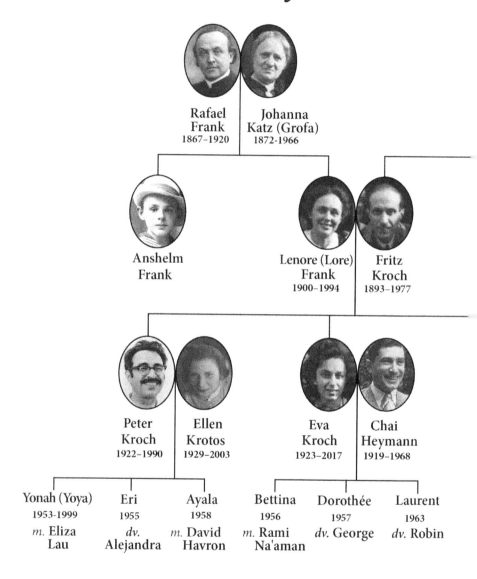

Rafael Frank 1867-1920 — Johanna Katz (Grofa) 1872-1966

Anshelm Frank

Lenore (Lore) Frank 1900-1994 — Fritz Kroch 1893-1977

Peter Kroch 1922-1990 — Ellen Krotos 1929-2003

Eva Kroch 1923-2017 — Chai Heymann 1919-1968

Yonah (Yoya) 1953-1999 *m.* Eliza Lau

Eri 1955 *dv.* Alejandra

Ayala 1958 *m.* David Havron

Bettina 1956 *m.* Rami Na'aman

Dorothée 1957 *dv.* George

Laurent 1963 *dv.* Robin

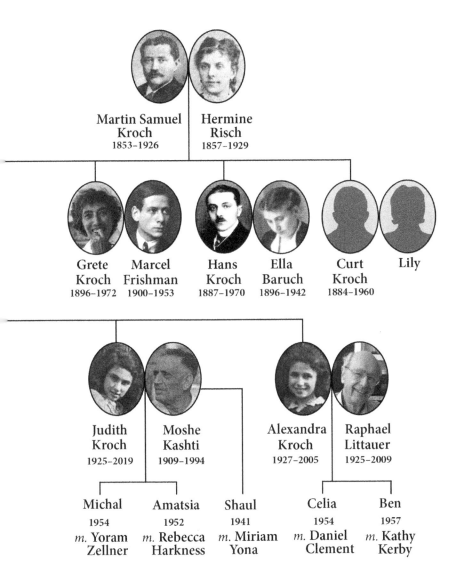

Martin Samuel Kroch
1853–1926

Hermine Risch
1857–1929

Grete Kroch
1896–1972

Marcel Frishman
1900–1953

Hans Kroch
1887–1970

Ella Baruch
1896–1942

Curt Kroch
1884–1960

Lily

Judith Kroch
1925–2019

Moshe Kashti
1909–1994

Alexandra Kroch
1927–2005

Raphael Littauer
1925–2009

Michal
1954
m. Yoram Zellner

Amatsia
1952
m. Rebecca Harkness

Shaul
1941
m. Miriam Yona

Celia
1954
m. Daniel Clement

Ben
1957
m. Kathy Kerby

For simplicity, only those family members who are mentioned in the story have been included in this family tree. Fritz had four other siblings. And his siblings who were included in the tree (Grete, Hans, and Curt) all had children who were left off the tree.

Germany, Belgium, and France: early 1940s

The locations indicated are those relevant to the Kroch story.

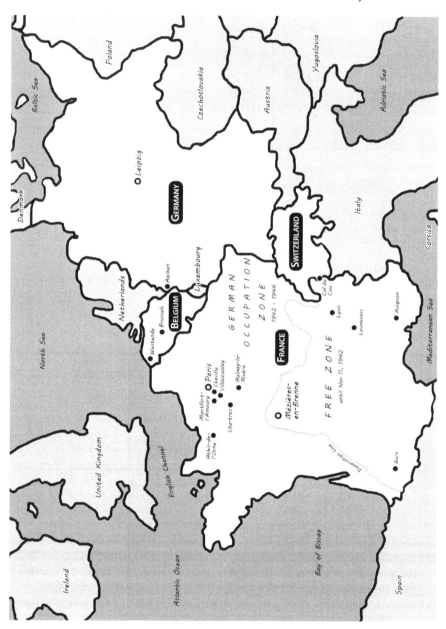

Prologue

My mother, Alexandra, always believed that she was lucky. Maman was perfectly happy with her life and often said so. I never heard her complain, though she lived with chronic back pain. It wasn't until much later that I really understood how she came to believe she was inherently lucky.

She was tough and outspoken, tiny and fragile, very self-confident, and very grounded. Many of her friends and family sought her for support and guidance. But because she was often sick, and often anxious, we all felt a need to protect her. Above all, she was warm and loving and avoided conflict of any kind. She provided a home full of calm and stability.

As a child, I didn't know of the harrowing experiences that had shattered her childhood. She kept them hidden because she wanted to forget and move on with her life and didn't want me or my brother, Ben, to be burdened by her trauma. Gradually, as I grew older, she shared the memories of her escape from Germany.

With enough distance from that horrific time, she was ready to remember and recount. She told her stories without emotional attachment. They were spellbinding and frightening, and not in any particular order. They were disjointed and surreal, as though she were talking about someone else.

"Would you let me record your stories?" I asked her one day, long after I was married and had moved out of our family home. She immediately agreed, pleased that I was interested. But I procrastinated, and when she became sick with cancer and almost died, I thought that I'd lost my chance. When she recovered, I realized that I'd been given a second chance to record her stories.

We met every day during the summer of 2003. She had her spot, nestled on a lounge chair propped up by her tropical fish pillows. Her small frame had shrunk even more, the result of her illness. She looked particularly vulnerable as she punctuated her words with deep drags from her cigarette. As we lounged on her sunny veranda overlooking Cayuga Lake, I taped the interviews. We were always very close, but during those moments I basked in the special intimacy that we had created. Her first grandchild, Ariana, spent the following summer filling in the missing pieces of her story, and then transcribed all the interviews.

Two years later I lost my mother.

Both Judith and Eva had written their own accounts of the Holocaust. I visited them in Israel during the summer of 2016 to hear more details of their experiences. I received their blessing to write this book, a weaving of the three sisters' stories. It was to be Eva's last summer. She died April 3, 2017, just shy of her 94th birthday. Two years later Judith died at the age of 94.

Memories are like clouds that warp and morph with time. They dance in our minds, changing, vanishing, and sometimes reappearing. Some memories are buried in our subconscious, never to be seen again. Other memories define and shape our characters. A distant memory rarely looks similar to people who have experienced the exact same event.

The sisters recounted their stories from their own perspectives. Each navigated the trauma as best she could, from the vantage point of her age, personality, and inner resources. Events affected each differently. The Kroch sisters responded to their hardships as children, and as adults making sense of what was happening from the viewpoint of a child, and then distilling and recalculating as adults. Against incredible odds, they survived along with their brother, Peter, their parents, Lore and Fritz, and their grandmother Grofa. These are the memories of the three sisters, woven together to tell the story of the Kroch family's escape from the Holocaust. They were the lucky ones.

Alexandra at her lakehouse

The three sisters: Judith, Eva, and Alexandra

THREE SISTERS

Chapter One
Kristallnacht, November 1938

Adolf Hitler's dramatic political ascendance began when he was elected the leader of the right-wing National Socialist German Workers Party (Nazi Party). By 1933 it had become one of the strongest political factions in Germany, even though the Nazis had won only 33 percent of the votes in the 1932 elections to the German parliament (Reichstag). On January 30th, 1933, Hitler was named chancellor, the most powerful position in the German government by the elderly President Hindenburg who hoped Hitler could guide the nation out of its serious political and economic crisis.

Once in power, Hitler's first agenda item was to end democracy. He convinced his cabinet to add emergency clauses into the constitution that allowed the suspension of individual freedoms of press, speech, and assembly. Special security forces: the Gestapo, the Storm Troopers (SA), and the SS (Schutzstaffel) — murdered or arrested leaders of opposition political parties (Communists, Socialists, and Liberals). Once his opponents were out of the way, Hitler decreed The Enabling Act of March 23, 1933, which gave him dictatorial powers. He no longer needed to go through the cabinet to enact laws and mandates. In 1933, the Nazis began to put their racial ideology into practice. The Nazis believed that the German (Aryan) race was pure and superior, and that there was no room in Germany for inferior "races" such as Jews or Gypsies, nor for people with disabilities.

On September 15, 1935, the Nuremberg laws were enacted which prohibited Jews from marrying anyone with non-Jewish ancestry. They defined being "Jewish" not by religious belief, but by lineage. You were a member of the Jewish "race" no matter what your conviction or identification. If you had at least three grandparents who were Jewish, you were considered Jewish, even if you were not a practicing Jew or had converted to another religion. The Nazis also spread hate-mongering propaganda that unfairly blamed Jews for Germany's economic depression and the country's defeat in World War I. Inflation had thrown many Germans into financial ruin. Jews who often enjoyed *a more affluent lifestyle became the obvious scapegoats.*[1]

On November 9 and 10, 1938, the Nazis instigated a riot (pogrom), known as Kristallnacht (the "Night of Broken Glass"). Jewish homes, hospitals, and schools were ransacked, and buildings were demolished. This attack against German Jews included the physical destruction of synagogues and Jewish-owned stores and the arrest of 30,000 men who were sent to concentration camps. Two hundred and sixty seven synagogues were burned and over 7,000 Jewish businesses were either destroyed or damaged.[2]

Most German Jews had been proud to be citizens of a country that had produced many great Jewish poets, writers, musicians, scientists, and artists. These families had considered Germany their home for generations. More than 100,000 German Jews had served in the German army during World War I, and of those, 12,000 Jewish soldiers were killed in action and 18,000 were awarded the Iron Cross for bravery.[3]

They could not fathom that their country would turn on them. The loss of their rights, the loss of their citizenship, the attacks on their homes, religion, livelihoods, and their lives was astonishing and horrifying.

On that night, the Kroch family suffered at the hands of the ruthless, vengeful Nazis as did every other Jewish family living in Germany. Eva, the eldest sister, was living away from her family when the Nazis stormed into her rooming house. Judith, the middle daughter, and Alexandra the youngest, were both living at home in Leipzig, Germany with their parents. Each girl remembers vividly the moment when everything changed.

Alexandra (Age 11)

The story is called: "Why I don't believe in God anymore." That was when I was eleven, and it was the night when the Gestapo came into our home. We lived on the fourth floor, and Uncle Curt lived on the second floor. The Gestapo thumped on his door, and we all woke up. There was a lot of commotion and shouting and we went to the window and saw Uncle Curt in his nightshirt being dragged across the street to a Volkswagen into which he was bundled together with two huge guys and a driver, and driven off. In my head I saw clearly that if my uncle could be treated that way, by those he called his "own people," for no purpose, for no reason – he had not committed any crime, he had not done anything wrong – then there was either a bad God, a mean God, or there was no God. And the choice was made; I didn't want to believe in a mean God. That very instant I thought; "Only a mean God would allow that – there is no mean God – there is no God."

Judith (Age 14)

During the times of extreme antisemitism in Germany, a young Jew by the name of Herschel Grynspan shot a German official in Paris on November 7th, 1938 to protest the deportation of his parents to Poland. This event became the pretext for the Kristallnacht on November 9, 1938. Even before the news had spread around the world, a well-planned action was set in motion organized by the Nazi party. All over Germany synagogues were torched, display windows of Jewish businesses were smashed, and stores were burnt to the ground. Some Jewish owners were sent to concentration camps where these bewildered and terrified people were beaten and threatened with death until they transferred all their belongings to the Nazis.

In the grey light of dawn on November 10, 1938 we were awakened by loud screams that sounded like the bellowing of an animal. These came from my Uncle Curt, whom the Gestapo had pulled out of bed. They pushed him brutally down the stairs in his nightshirt and Curt screamed so frightfully that his voice had lost all human quality. He was

3

howling in protest and disbelief. He, the blameless German lawyer and notary, was being arrested like a common criminal. Even a criminal is given time to put a coat over his nightshirt. But the Jew Kroch was torn from his home without any explanation and beaten because he tried to defend himself. They forced him into a waiting car as his wife ran after him screaming, "Help, help!" But no one could help them.

Our mother was alone with us because our father and Peter, our brother, were in France to prepare for our immigration there. Then our telephone rang. It was the Gestapo asking my mother where my father was. She was in shock, and so were we all. We could still hear the echoes of those desperate screams. When she explained that Fritz Kroch was abroad, my mother was told in no uncertain terms that he had to return immediately, or else she would be picked up instead. This threat was unfortunately only too believable.

The news that Fritz's other brother, Uncle Hans, had also been arrested reached us quickly. At a time when there was no radio in our house ("Because the children will stop doing their homework," my father explained) the telephone was our means of communication. Frightened women with shaking voices whispered the essentials into the telephone. Thus, we heard that almost all our relatives had suffered the same fate. They had been arrested just as brutally as Curt and Hans.

We lived in a part of town where there were no stores, and therefore we had not heard the shattering of glass from the smashed display windows. As unbelievable as it may sound, our faithful chauffeur came to drive us to school the next day. Even more astounding is that our mother permitted it. But she was in deep shock and hardly knew what was happening around her. When we arrived at school, the building had been burnt down. There were only a few bewildered children standing around. I was worried about my younger sister and my even smaller cousin and took them home. By the time we got home, our mother had already been admitted to the Jewish hospital. Her nerves could not cope with the harrowing events of the night. This hospital was under Polish protection and could not be entered by German police.

Our grandmother, Johanna Frank, whom everyone called Grofa, took us to her apartment. Her family name was not linked to ours, so we felt relatively secure there. Hans and Curt, after their arrest, were sent to the camps Sachsenhausen and Buchenwald and were freed in January 1939, only after every family member had signed papers renouncing all claims to the family fortune, including the Kroch-Bank and all of its assets.

Eva (Age 15)

I lived in Mrs. Neuberger's boarding house, in Würzburg while I attended a Jewish teaching seminary. Our apartment was shaped like the letter resh (ר). The corner room could easily be missed, and this was her best room. There Mrs. Neuberger had her finest furniture, crystal glassware, and precious wall hangings. None of us were allowed in there. Just once did I have the privilege of being permitted to have a quick look. There was one dining room that doubled as a living room, and the rest of the rooms were used as bedrooms for the tenants. Mrs. Neuberger's mother also occupied a small room, which was next to mine.

On November 9, we went to sleep quite normally. Suddenly at about 11 at night there was a banging at the door, then crashing noises. The Germans broke the door down with an axe and entered. Mrs. Neuberger came into my room, and I put her into my bed. She wasn't much over 70, but at 70 she seemed ancient. She was terrified and mumbled prayers. The Germans smashed the windows and pictures in my room. Everything was covered with glass splinters, including my bed and the face of Mrs. Neuberger. The Germans threatened to kill her if she did not keep quiet. I put my hand over her mouth, hoping that I wasn't cutting her with glass splinters.

One German stood in front of me with an axe. He kept bringing the axe down over my head but didn't touch my head. "Laugh, you Jew swine! Why are you laughing at me, you Jew swine? I am going to split your head in two!" I always was, and am today, terribly afraid of mutilation. I was so afraid that he would cut off my nose or my ear. The Germans were there to terrify, and this they did. The old woman was in shock and could not stop making noises, and so I again pressed my hand on her mouth and hoped that I wasn't suffocating her. I prayed he would bring the axe down straight on my head. "Now! Now! And then it's over!" Then suddenly he was gone.

The house itself was a strong building and had not been destroyed, but outside the pavement was covered with smashed furniture. Everything in the house was in ruins. Everything except the corner room! If they'd known what wonderful things were in the corner room … but they had missed it! We were so happy about that. There is a Jewish proverb that says, "If you pull a hair out of a pig, it's a mitzvah (good deed)." Not nice for the poor pig, but we felt we'd pulled a hair out of the German pigs.

In the Teachers' Seminary, everything had been destroyed. Furniture and books had been broken and burnt. The pupils had to go home, but I could not leave immediately. My father was in Paris, and my mother was in the hospital. So, I had to wait until somebody came to fetch me. Soon our Jewish maid, Bienchen, blond and blue-eyed, came to get me from Würzburg, and we took the train back home to my family in Leipzig.

The Boerneplatz synagogue in flames during the Kristallnacht pogrom, Frankfurt am Main, Germany, November 10, 1938

Courtesy of US Holocaust Memorial Museum

Jewish men arrested during Kristallnacht are forced to march through the town streets under SS guard and to watch the desecration of a synagogue before their deportation.

Courtesy of US Holocaust Memorial Museum, Lydia Chagol

Chapter Two
Germany: Life Before World War II
1918-1936

Jews represented only one percent of the German population during the time leading up to 1933; however, they enjoyed a disproportionately high share of the prosperity. Many of the large businesses were owned by Jews, including department stores, banks, iron, steel and coal industries, textiles, and newspapers. Jews held important positions in government and taught in Germany's renowned universities. Of the 38 Nobel Prizes awarded to German writers and scientists between 1905 and 1936, 14 recipients were Jews. The Jewish citizenry had a large presence in the legal, medical, educational, and economic systems of the country.[3]

Martin Samuel Kroch, my great-grandfather, was born in 1857. During the early 1870s, while in his 20s, he founded his banking and grain businesses. When grain became unprofitable at the end of the century, he liquidated that business and moved into real estate.

A very successful businessman, he later modestly explained, "I didn't make my money through wisdom, but with luck. Rising real estate prices – that was my luck." He was also known to be very frugal. When traveling by train, he would purchase a third-class ticket, though he could have easily afforded to travel first class.

He would proudly explain, "I can travel just as fast for less money." And, though he was very frugal with his own family needs, he was known to contribute generously to charitable causes.

He and his wife, Hermine, had eight children. Two died before reaching adulthood, and one emigrated to Australia. Curt, the eldest son, became a lawyer. Hans took over the family banking and real estate businesses. Grete, the youngest child, became an accomplished artist and lived a bohemian lifestyle with her husband Marcel and son Martin. Fritz, born in 1893, was the fifth child and my grandfather.

Martin Samuel and Hermine Kroch were religious Jews, but they were also quite progressive. Fritz used the word "enlightened" to describe his parents. He recalled a conversation with his mother,

7

who told him, "Just because a man goes to the synagogue, he is not necessarily religious. To do good is what makes a man religious."

"Papa Fritz," as we called my grandfather, excelled in his studies. After finishing his schooling, he joined his family business and then served in the cavalry on the French border. He was discharged in 1918 after having been decorated with an Iron Cross. He returned to Leipzig and took over his father's refrigeration business.

Papa Fritz was a remarkably unattractive man, 5 feet three inches tall with a very prominent nose and large, protruding front teeth. But this is not what one noticed. What stood out about Fritz was his warm, twinkling personality and sharp wit. He particularly enjoyed debating philosophical subjects with his family and friends, such as the consideration of determinism versus free will. As a young child, what I most remember about my jokester grandfather was the silly sounds he would make to entertain his grandchildren and the delicious chocolate pastries he would buy from down the street to be served with afternoon tea.

Papa Fritz's wife, my grandmother Lore, descended from a much more modest background. Her grandparents, Isaac Katz and Helene Fiorino, lived in Kassel, Germany, where Isaac made a living as a merchant who sold grain, feathers, and wool. He and Helene had three beautiful daughters. Ida, the eldest, was blond. Johanna, the brunette, whom we all called Grofa, was my great-grandmother. And the youngest, Selma, had jet black hair.

One day, when the girls were still young, Isaac Katz disappeared. Grofa never found out what happened to him, and her mother never mentioned her husband again. Her sisters, Selma and Ida, married two brothers, Max and Wilhelm Lande. Both men were to play a role in the lives and escapes of the Krochs.

The brothers couldn't have been more different; Max was a kind man, and Wilhelm was pathologically jealous, and a womanizer. The brothers came from a very large, poor family in Lithuania. Wilhelm, the elder brother, left home when he was a teenager to make his fortune in Germany. Max ran away from home when he was fourteen and walked on his own, a long and dangerous journey, to join his brother. The two started a business making gold-tipped cigarettes for military officers and soon did well enough to open a large factory in Dresden.

Max and Wilhelm did not get along and often fought bitterly. Max moved his family to Zurich, where he opened his own factory and became a very wealthy man. During World War II, he helped support many Jews, including the Krochs. He often gave away his money anonymously.

My great-grandmother Johanna (Grofa) married Rafael Frank, the son of an antique dealer from Swabia, a region of southern Germany. The Franks were intellectuals who opened their home to many gatherings of musicians, artists, scholars, and scientists. Rafael played piano and violin, and sang. Though Rafael began to study voice professionally, the lack of financial resources forced him instead to become a teacher and cantor.

Rafael was also a gifted artist and was commissioned to design a modern Hebrew character font. Named "Frank-Ruhl-Hebrew," it continues to be the most widely used print of the Hebrew language. Grofa and Rafael had two children: Anshelm and my grandmother Lore, who was born in 1900. A strikingly beautiful girl, Lore, like her father, was a very talented musician who sang and accompanied herself on the piano. She spent years studying to be an opera singer. Lore was gentle and kind, an introvert who preferred to sit back and let her family take center stage.

In 1920, Lore married Fritz Kroch. Just before they married, Fritz's mother, Helene, whispered to his future bride, my grandmother Lore: "You are getting the best one. My little Fritz is pure love."

Alexandra

My father, Fritz, was to be betrothed to a young woman named Mimi, who had been found suitable by his family. In order for them to meet, he was invited to a very large party of important people from the Jewish community in Leipzig. Fritz was walking from room to room looking for Mimi when he entered a room and saw in the alcove a very beautiful young girl who was playing the lute and singing with a beautiful voice. My father joined the crowd of young men gathered around her and stopped looking for Mimi. His first thought was "I want to marry that girl." And that girl was my mother, Lore, whom we all called Mutti, which means "mommy." She was barely eighteen, and he was seven years older. She was the most renowned beauty of that crowd. And he was known as a member of one of the richest families in Leipzig.

Fritz went to my mother's house a few days later with a great bouquet of flowers, and when my grandmother came to the door and said, "Oh, Herr Kroch, you shouldn't have," he replied, "It's not for you, it's for your daughter."

He also one time brought Lore a large, very expensive art book. Mutti asked, "How did you know I'm interested in this?"

He responded, "Oh, I didn't, I just picked the biggest book and bought it."

For a year he pursued my mother, who didn't want anything to do with him. Although she thought him nice, he was too ugly and too rich. Her mother, "Grofa," had explained that if she, the most beautiful girl, was going to marry this man, all her friends would say she married him for his money alone, and they would all drop her as a friend.

Toward the end of 1919, my mother became very sick with an ear infection. She was in the hospital for a very long time, and nearly died. My father visited her in the hospital every day. When she was not in the mood for company, he would sit down in her room and say nothing, just be there. And if she wanted something to drink or anything, he would bring it to her. He sat quietly and took care of her. My mother told me that after she was back home and was again well, she could not imagine a life without this man. They were married in November 1920. Most of Lore's friends in Leipzig did, in fact, step away from her. Grofa was quite right.

Peter was born in 1922, Eva in 1923, Judith in 1924, and I in 1927. We never lived in a big mansion; that was Uncle Hans's. My father didn't believe in owning real estate. He felt that as a Jew he shouldn't own land; he should be free.

We always had servants, but we treated them as part of the family. Miss Lock from England was hired to teach my older siblings English. Werner, the chauffeur, was employed by the Kroch bank and provided the transportation for both our family and Hans's family. He was a rotund person with a very shiny, hairless scalp and a very strong

Saxon accent. Hedi, short for Hedwich, was the cook. She was a big woman, at least to me, since I was a very small girl. We had a very skinny and very nice chambermaid, but I do not remember her name. She and Hedi shared a room behind the kitchen in the Mozart Strasse 23, where we lived opposite the park. We also had a governess; the only one I remember was Erna, because she was hired at a time that my memory begins. She had a nice round face, and was average in every way, height, weight, and beauty. There was nothing outstanding about her looks, only about her character and her intelligence.

After a while, Jews were not allowed to hire non-Jewish servants. And eventually we only had one servant, a maid called Martha. She was well over 45, very tall and broad with long black hair, and very made-up, with a lot of lipstick and rouge. She looked like a gypsy. I remember when beggars came to the front door, she would give them a cup of coffee and a bowl of soup to eat outside the house. When they were finished, they would return the bowl and cup, and go on their way. Some of them asked for and received seconds.

One day, one of them kept coming back for more, and after his thirds, Martha got very upset with him. When he kept ringing the front doorbell one too many times, Martha went to the front door with a little paring knife in her hand, which she held like a dagger.

And she said, "If you don't leave now, I'm taking this knife, and I will kill you." And she said it in such a way that he didn't come back. She looked pretty frightening when she wanted to.

During the week, we didn't eat with our parents because they had their own schedules. My mother ran the household. She had singing lessons and practiced her music. When my siblings were out, I had no one to play with. I sat under the grand piano and looked at comic books while my mother practiced scales. When my brother and sisters and I played together, Peter was the leader; he proposed and supervised the games. There were four of us born in five and a half years, so we were a very cohesive group. Even though I was the youngest, in many ways I was in the middle of Eva and Judith. When we stayed in a room together, Judith was messy, Eva was a neat freak, and I was in between. Eva had her head in the clouds, Judith had her feet firmly on the ground, and I was in the middle.

We played one game when we were vacationing in Aix-en-Provence in 1933. We stayed in Le Chateau Noir, and it had a park all around it. Peter built a garden for all the animals: all the frogs, snakes, snails, and caterpillars we could find. Our garden was made of petals and moss, and it was quite extensive. Peter created it, and then sent Eva, Judith, and me to find all the necessary building materials and animals.

My mother told me many years later that she had asked Peter how he had persuaded his sisters to run around getting him these things.

Peter had grinned, as he often did, and replied, "I told Judith, you bring the best snails. And I told Eva, only you can find these pebbles. And I told Edzie (which was my name as a child, and no one, including me, knows where it came from), I don't know how you find this moss, it's amazing!" And it worked. We loved to do it.

When I was very small, about four or five years old, we had a new nursemaid. It was her first day, and my parents went out for our dinner. We used to have a rule that we had to taste everything that was served. We had to have a teaspoonful. That night, dinner was red cabbage, which I absolutely hated.

So, when the maid served us, I said, "I only want a teaspoon full; I don't like it."

And the nursemaid retorted, "Children eat everything that's on their plates," and gave me a great big plop of cabbage.

I insisted, "I'll eat everything else, but I'll only eat a teaspoonful of cabbage." And that's what I did.

The nursemaid persisted, "You have to eat all of it." And I said "no," and she said "yes," and I said "no." So, she picked me up and trapped my arms with her left arm, and force fed me red cabbage. As soon as she had finished with the cabbage, I ran to the bathroom and spit up. I was very miserable.

When my mother came home, I told her the whole story. My mother said it was her own fault that she hadn't explained the rules properly to the new maid. And to make up for the misery, I would never have to eat red cabbage – even the teaspoonful – from now on. However, a few years later, in Paris after the war, I came into the Hotel du Commerce one day, and I smelled a fantastically good smell.

When I came into my parents' room, I said to my mother,

"There's a wonderful smell here. What are you cooking?"

And she grinned and said, "Red cabbage – do you want to taste it?" And I have loved it ever since.

Judith

My parents were wealthy, very wealthy. But we children were unaware of this. I thought money was bought at the Kroch-Bank like bread at the bakery. When we were still very small, we had four or five employees in our household. There was a chambermaid, a chauffeur and the cook named Hedwig who worked for us for a long time, and Erna, the governess for the older children. There was also a licensed infant nurse for the babies. The window cleaner came periodically, and twice a month we had a laundress who attacked and vanquished mountains of dirty linen in the laundry room.

As children we were taught discipline and obedience. The Sabbath was the day of rest. One went to the synagogue in one's best clothes. No drawing, writing or playing records. The Sabbath was reserved solely for spiritual and intellectual pursuits. Accompanied by our Erna, we usually walked through the Johanna Park to Sebastian Bach Strasse and our uncle's house with its private synagogue. We were not allowed to bring anything because it is forbidden to carry things on the Sabbath. And so with our handkerchiefs tied around our wrists we trotted past the two ponds, carefree and happy. It would never have occurred to us to eat outside the home, or to ask for an ice-cream in the park since it was said to contain gelatin made of un-kosher bone marrow. All non-kosher foods were repugnant to us.

Hedwig, well-padded as behooves a cook, had very quickly learnt all the complicated dietary laws laid down by the Jewish religion, though she was not Jewish. Werner, the chauffeur, faithfully served the family. Since the Jewish school was quite a distance from our home, he took the children there in the morning and picked us up again at lunchtime. Around nine o'clock he drove the men of the house, Uncle Curt and my father, to the "shop" (which was not a shop at all, but a general expression for business).

Our apartment had elegantly carpeted stairs which led to an entrance decorated in red and black. There was a hall with a billiard table in the middle and still plenty of space all around it. Set into the window wall was a bright alcove with several leather armchairs. A corridor led to the bedrooms, the bathroom, two toilets, and a special little room for washing hands. At the end of the corridor there were the kitchen and the pantry leading into the maid's room. In earlier days the cooking was still done on a big, coal-fed, cast-iron stove. Later a stove was installed, fueled by city gas. But the big old stove remained in the kitchen, just in case.

My parents' room was next to their three daughters' bedroom. My brother, Peter, had his own room. In the playroom there stood a blue rustic wardrobe with colorfully decorated doors. For us, the outstanding feature of our playroom was the gramophone. It was quite modern, and we were allowed to put the records on by ourselves.

Off the big entrance hall was the study, always smelling a little of cigar smoke, which contained our parents' precious library, a large desk and a number of comfortable armchairs. The dining room had two raised alcoves, and in one of these my parents ate breakfast. In the center of the room was a dining table that seated twenty-four. There were also a sideboard and a cabinet; all this on an immense Persian carpet. Only on the Sabbath and High Holidays were the children allowed to eat here with our parents. Usually we were served our meals in the playroom.

I hated these occasions when we dined with our parents at the festive, elegantly set dinner table. My father was a teacher at heart and could not refrain from giving us problems to solve during the meal. Sometimes we were given a letter to compose on a topic of his choice, or we had to demonstrate our knowledge of geography. But by far the worst was arithmetic, mental computation at the dinner table. It was so embarrassing when we made a fool of ourselves. Sometimes we were given a hint, but the food didn't taste good anymore.

Next to the dining room, half encircling the hall was the music room, with sofa and armchairs upholstered in blue velvet, walls covered in blue satin, billowing draperies around the semi-circular windows, and a splendid Steinway grand piano.

Eva

In our large music room, my mother would sometimes sing to an audience of fifteen to twenty people: family, friends, and business colleagues of my father. We couldn't hear her from our rooms, where we lived our own lives. My mother studied singing in Leipzig for many years. She was a mezzo soprano and was working towards her high C.

When I was six, we moved to Lugano, Italy, for six months while my mother studied singing in Milan at the Scala. We went swimming every day at the Lido. On the way to the beach we wore our beach suits. They were overalls with wide-bottomed trouser legs made of pretty, light, colorful material with straps or a bow at the shoulders. These suits were dressy enough for us to wear as we walked around the resort, with our wide brimmed matching hats starched with strong linen that made "waves" around our heads. We had a nursemaid, Gerda, who went with us. She sat on the beach and kept an eye on the four children.

On a particular day that I remember, Mutti was with us. She was an excellent swimmer and had once crossed Lake Lucerne, swimming for two hours with a boat close by.

She wanted us to learn how to swim and, on that day, announced, "I'm the best teacher for my children." She took me in her arms, turned her back to the lake and began to teach me to swim in the shallow water. I made the movements, and as I turned around, I suddenly saw Judith quite far out. Her head was bobbing up and down in the water.

I yelled to my mother, "Look at the water, Judith's head keeps coming up and going down." My mother turned around and had the worst moment of her life. She could neither run nor swim in the shallow water, so she jumped like a stork to get into deeper water and caught Judith by the head and pulled her out. She had to turn Judith upside down because she was full of water.

The nursemaid sat on her chair and read a book and had no idea what was going on. She only became aware when people came running to help Mutti hold Judith upside down and shake her. I don't remember if she was unconscious, but she lay there apathetically. After this experience Judith hated water, and it was very admirable that she forced herself to learn to swim when she was older. Of course, the nursemaid who had been with us for two years was told to pack her things, and she left the next day.

My father encouraged his wife to take singing lessons, but when she had become good enough to sing professionally, he told her. "I cannot have a wife, the mother of my four children, who is always travelling." She decided to give up her career as a singer for love of her husband and family, and I never knew if she completely came to terms with her decision.

My mother once told me that she herself had passed from the good hands of her parents into the good hands of her husband. My father adored her, and she did not mind the fact that he dominated her. I believe that my mother was very self-confident. People who allow themselves to be so dominated without thinking, "He is making me small," don't feel that they are being diminished. I see this as a strength and think that people who have to prove their worth are ones who feel inferior. My mother had no feelings of inferiority because she was extraordinarily beautiful and had been much loved and appreciated by her family, had good friends, and was a good pupil. She was unbelievably patient and gentle and had a good sense of humor. I seldom saw her angry.

One day when I was quite young, I came home from school and complained to my mother that one of my friends had a new governess, and another one had a new mother. I told her that I wanted something new, too. So, a few days later I woke up from my afternoon nap and the door opened and my mother came in with a new governess, who had a mustache and wore an immense coat and an immense hat.

In a very gruff voice she announced, "I am the new governess."

I was so scared that I cried, "I want my Erna. I want my old governess again." To teach me a lesson, my mother had asked Erna to dress up as the "new governess."

I liked many subjects, but I was a "bad" student. I stopped listening as soon as a teacher did not interest me, as soon as I was bored. I then retreated into dreams and was in fact absent from the classroom.

When a teacher asked, "Eva, what did I say?"

I answered quite simply and truthfully, "I don't know."

I was not an insecure child. I never lied or looked for excuses, and I wasn't embarrassed. If the teacher reacted angrily, I again retreated into my own world, standing with eyes downcast as the situation demanded. I was always able to escape into dreams, and this continued into adulthood. Later, in prison, this escape into dreams made it possible for me to avoid feeling sorry for myself.

I continued to be unhappy at school and had bad grades. When I was almost twelve, my mother told me that if I wanted to leave, she'd find me another school. So, I moved to Würzburg, Bavaria, where I eventually attended a Jewish seminary for teachers. Since I was still too young for the teaching seminary, I attended a preparatory school nearby and lived with my grandfather's brother. He had a grocery store, and I was very spoiled. I later went to live in a boarding house with two other students. It wasn't hard for me to leave home because I liked new adventures. I knew bad things could happen, but I didn't think they would happen to me.

*Grofa's mother Helene Fiorino with her
three daughters: Ida, Selma, and
Johanna (Grofa)*

*Johanna (Grofa) and
Rafael Frank, 1896*

*Grofa with her two children:
Anshelm and Lore, 1910*

Fritz's parents Martin Samuel Kroch and Hermine M. Risch Kroch, 1883

Lore and Fritz Kroch

Krochhochhaus (Kroch Bank) Leipszig, Germany
commons.wikimedia.org/wiki/File:Leipzig_-_Krochhochhaus.jpg

Fritz and Lore Kroch

*Lore and Nanny at the beach with
Peter, Eva, Judith, and Alexandra*

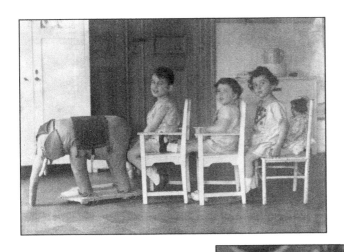

Kroch children

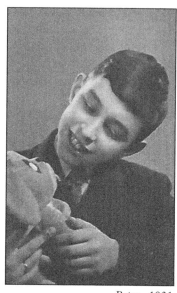

Peter, 1931

*Lore with her children
Peter, Judith, Eva, and
Alexandra Kroch, 1929*

*Kroch children
out for a stroll*

Chapter Three
Antisemitism

"The Jewish Problem" [4] *was an expression introduced in order to begin the process of changing people's perceptions of Jews. Once Jews were identified as a problem, the next step was to find a solution. Hitler promoted himself as the leader who was going to solve "The Jewish Problem." In order to reinforce loyalty to himself and the Nazi party, a salute was created. When Germans greeted each other, they were expected to jump to attention with their arms raised straight ahead while shouting, "Heil Hitler." Parades organized by Hitler's militia, marched through neighborhoods frequently, and often without forewarning. Onlookers who failed to salute were at risk of being beaten.*

Hitler began his campaign of enacting decrees that would solve "The Jewish Problem." Beginning in 1933, laws were increasingly passed that took away the rights and freedoms of German Jews. The intent was to humiliate, stigmatize, and clearly identify Jews in order to segregate them from the rest of society. Increasingly, Jews were ousted from their careers. Nazis either seized Jewish businesses and properties outright or forced Jews to sell their businesses at considerably below their value.

Jews were barred from attending public schools or universities and forbidden to reside in or stroll through certain neighborhoods. They were prohibited from attending plays or concerts, owning phones, owning land, or driving cars. Books written by Jews were burned. Jews were eventually victims of more than 400 decrees and regulations that deprived them of their rights and freedom, and restricted all aspects of their public and private lives.

Beginning in 1938, Jewish men and women with first names that were not obviously Jewish had to add "Israel" and "Sarah," respectively, to their given names and were required to carry identity cards at all times. All Jewish passports were stamped with the letter "J." And in 1941, it was decreed that all Jews over age six were required to wear a badge which consisted of a yellow Star of David imprinted with the word "JUDE." These acts of antisemitism were intended to identify and stigmatize Jews and to reinforce their inferior status.

Once Jews were stripped of their rights, they were left vulnerable to arbitrary arrest, incarceration, torture, and murder. Members of the Gestapo (the secret state police, fiercely loyal to Hitler) were the primary perpetrators of the terror and control of German citizens. They were carefully trained to be detached and sadistic, and relied on a network of informants. A systematic and thorough ideology steadily infiltrated every aspect of German culture which insured that everyone would be a member of the Jewish eradication plan. Every non-Jewish citizen was expected and required to denounce Jews for any reason, or for no reason. Informants were commended, and those protecting Jews were punished.

At age five or six, non-Jewish children were obligated to go to Nazi training camps to begin the carefully orchestrated process of indoctrination. They were fed negative information about Jews, while simultaneously being groomed to be faithful Nazi disciples. This finely tuned brainwashing machine ensured that everyone would turn against the Jews and ultimately assist Hitler in his "final solution" to the "Jewish Problem" which was to kill every Jewish man, woman, and child. [5]

The Kroch sisters were increasingly confronted with the loss of rights and with situations that changed their relationships with their neighbors and threatened their safety.

Judith

When Hitler came to power, he needed a scapegoat to blame for all the hardships in Germany. To begin with there was the Treaty of Versailles, which the vanquished Germany had been forced to sign at the end of the First World War. Germany lost all its colonies and went through a period of severe economic deprivation. Communists, too, were the enemy of the Third Reich, as Hitler, the megalomaniac, called Germany. And the Jews were seen as being ultimately responsible. How convenient. When food or foreign currency was scarce, when the cost of living escalated, or the winter was too cold, who was to blame? The

Jews. This way the government was never to blame. More and more Germans began to believe in the hate propaganda against the Jews.

The word "antisemitism," which I occasionally heard in grown-ups' conversation, had no meaning for me. I understood that we, as Jews, were unfairly discriminated against just for being Jewish. But this had no noticeable influence on our daily lives. We read the same fairy tales as all the other children, adored the same movie stars, collected the same set of pictures that had to be glued into special albums, and listened to our father's recollections of the First World War.

The first sign of unrest in my life began one evening when gigantic steamer trunks were hastily packed in our playroom because a major confrontation between Communists and National Socialists was expected to take place in the neighboring Johanna Park the following day. It was feared that there would be violence and that one or the other party might well attack the homes of wealthy Jews. And so, we left that night by train for a spa in Carlsbad, Czechoslovakia. This spa catered to people suffering from constipation, for there are sources of saline waters in this scenic area that, when slowly sipped, produce dramatic results. There was a long promenade with fountains where ladies and gentlemen could fill their glasses and amble up and down slowly sipping through thin glass tubes. Every now and then one of them would disappear in a hurry into one of the little "houses" that lined the promenade.

During my childhood it was still considered unseemly to speak of digestion, and we were therefore highly amused when we saw the corpulent ladies and gentlemen, who had overeaten all year long and were so terribly proper, suddenly being taken by surprise, moving very quickly and vanishing abruptly.

At any rate, we were given colorful Bohemian glass goblets imprinted with our names, created before our eyes by local glass blowers.

We didn't stay long in Carlsbad, and soon we moved to Paris. There we lived in a very nice hotel on Boulevard Malesherbes where we occupied a suite. Our governess Alice was with us.

I was immediately fascinated by Paris. It is known as 'The City of Lights" for good reason. Leipzig was not a small city, but was so plain, uneventful, and bland compared to Paris, where the shops were chic and the Parisians were merry and well dressed, and in the manicured parks there were pools where little boys floated their sailboats.

Unfortunately, we could not stay in Paris for long because my father had to return to Leipzig for business reasons. What a contrast. There was no homecoming; it was a sad return to a cage, and not a gilded one. The National Socialist Party was not only a political party, but had become a lifestyle. Men in brown shirts marched bellowing, "Wenn's Judenblut vom Messer spritzt" (When Jewish blood squirts from the knife).

From the windows fluttered flags with swastikas, the bigger the better. By now we were grown up enough to detect the worry in our parents' voices. The situation of the Jews in Germany was becoming unbearable. Friends and acquaintances were emigrating. There was talk of Palestine. Our parents had been there in 1925 and had returned full of enthusiasm. But my father's brothers were against the division of the family fortune, which our emigration would necessitate. In addition, they, like so many other German Jews who had served as volunteers in the First World War, still hoped that this nightmare (the Nazi regime) would soon fade. At first there were whispers. Later it became common knowledge, loud and clear, that this person or that had been "taken away." Those who returned were distraught, did not want to talk, took bare necessities, left home and livelihood, and fled abroad with their families.

In light of what was happening to the Jews in Germany, our family moved into a house belonging to my father's elder brother Curt. As in all upper middle-class houses, there were a caretaker and his wife. We liked Herr and Frau Heller very much and for a while continued to play with their children Traute and Helmut. After a while the younger son, Gunther, did not want to associate with us "Jew-children." Later Helmut and Traute were afraid to play with us because Gunther might report us to the Hitlerjugend (the Nazi organization for boys).

From time to time, Herr Heller was summoned to serve in a military corps. He returned from one of these assignments and said to my father, "Herr Kroch, I am not allowed to tell you what I have seen. It is so dreadful that you should go abroad immediately." What exactly he meant by that I still don't know. Perhaps he had witnessed the beginning of what was being built for the annihilation of the Jewish people.

However, we did not leave immediately. The children continued to be driven to school every day. During recess we could no longer jump around happily and freely as we had done before, but instead had to walk around the schoolyard three abreast, moving slowly, listless, sadly, and keeping our voices down. The story was that the neighbors had complained about the noise from the "Jew-School." I doubt if the noise we'd made during the breaks was worse than in any other playground. But if it was Aryan noise, then it was permitted.

The playground was surrounded by high walls. One day as we were walking around in a circle, a figure appeared on the top of the wall and poured down boiling oil. A few children were burnt, but the school filed no charges since it would not have done any good. From then on, we were warned not to walk too close to the wall. Happy and carefree times were over forever. In school and out, there was a sense of oppression. We could not feel cheerful anymore. There was a latent fear in us.

On the early morning of 28 October 1938, a few days after my fourteenth birthday, the telephone rang, waking the entire family. The police had carried out an operation against all Jews of Polish nationality. The action had been triggered by a new Polish law that deprived Polish Jews of the right to return to Poland. Since Germany did not want these people, either, the police came to the homes of Polish Jewish families, many of whom were German-born Polish nationals. They were ordered out of bed and allowed to pack only a small suitcase, and then driven to the train station where hundreds of others were already amassed. The train brought them to the Polish border. They were not permitted to return to Germany. Yet in Poland they knew no one, had no money, didn't speak Polish and stood about stunned, wondering what to do next. There were rumors that at some border checkpoints Polish police fired on the involuntary immigrants. Most of these unfortunate people eventually died a miserable death after the Germans marched into Poland.

News of the operation against the Polish Jews immediately spread throughout the Jewish community, and most German Jews opened their homes to as many Polish-Jewish acquaintances as they could possibly accommodate. A phone call alerted us that we would be receiving a Polish family. Though our house was well heated, we shivered with nervous tension, for we had taken in a family of seven who had sought refuge with us. The atmosphere was somber since no one knew if our home would be searched for Polish Jews. One of the daughters was a classmate of mine. Her youngest sister chirped away merrily, quite unconcerned, and she made us all laugh.

The Polish consul in Leipzig took more than a thousand Polish citizens into the consulate under his protection, thereby saving them from deportation. Our Polish family later escaped to Israel. We did not dare go into the street until a few days later, when we heard that the Polish Operation had been completed. When we returned to school, several classmates were missing, as well as some of our teachers.

Alexandra

Her name was Traute, and we were best friends. Her mother and father were against Hitler, and her brothers were divided: the older one was against Hitler, and the younger one was for him. The boys were already in the Hitlerjugend; one against his better judgment and the other one all for it. Traute was six years old, a year older than I. Her mother didn't want to send her to Bund Deutscher Mädel (BDM: girls' wing of the Nazi Party youth movement). Children were supposed to start at five or six years old, and her mother was able to keep her out for a year with a phony health certificate from a doctor. But the following year the doctor was afraid to renew the certificate, and she had to go.

We had been playing together daily; we lived in the same house. Then came the day when she had to go to the BDM. I couldn't wait until she got back home to play. I was not permitted to cross the street, but I was allowed to walk along the sidewalk to the corner, which I did when I knew she was going to come home. I could see her coming from quite a way, and she passed me by without a look. I ran behind her, thinking "Of course she can't greet me in the street. I'm Jewish, she can't do that." So, when we had reached the house, I was convinced now we were going to be friends and start playing, but she never, ever spoke to me again, ever. That was my first experience with how the BDM could brainwash. It took only one day ... and I, Traute's Jewish friend, was no longer in existence. Never did she speak to me again, let alone play with me. But Traute's older brother snuck into my brother's room, and they were playmates, and he kept this up until we left.

Eva

We did have some Nazi teachers. One of them was particularly insulting. I remember a lesson we had about Africa when this teacher explained that in Africa "There are Blacks and Hottentots. Look, we have one in our class, small and black!" and he pointed at me. But fortunately, in our school we had something that I call "class spirit." Nobody wanted to be a part of an attack by a teacher. Everybody sat silently, faces stiff, the atmosphere cold. "Class spirit" excluded the teachers. They were not considered part of the class. We arranged things among ourselves. Perhaps one of the reasons for our rather grown up "class spirit" was that we were conscious of the period in which we were living and the dangers that surrounded us.

One day when I was walking home from school and just as I was about to cross the street to my house, Hitler came by in a motorcade, and there were people along the street with their hands up saluting him, shouting "Heil Hitler." I was so afraid that they would see me and realize that I was a Jewish girl. I don't know what they would have done to me. They would have been able to beat me to death. But they didn't notice me. They were too busy concentrating on Hitler standing up in his car. I remember the fear.

German   *French*

The policy of forcing Jews to wear badges was one of many tactics aimed at identifying, stigmatizing, and dehumanizing the Jews of Europe, thereby marking them as being different and inferior.

Holocaust Memorial Center: www.holocaustcenter.org

Chapter Four
Smuggled Out of Germany, November 1938

After Kristallnacht, all German Jews were abruptly propelled into a harsh new reality. The situation for the Kroch family had worsened overnight. The men of the family had been viciously removed from their homes, leaving the stunned women alone to figure out how to save their children. Lore was not able to cope with the stress and ended up in a psychiatric hospital. Grofa, her mother, was the one left to plan the escape of her three granddaughters. She contacted a smuggling ring that had sprung up to capitalize on the desperate need of Jews to escape Germany. These were paid, professional rescuers, who faced death if they were captured.

The three sisters had been carefully sheltered. They were unaware of the hastily unfolding plans. Grofa was about to place her grandchildren's lives into the hands of strangers. Eva, Judith, and Alexandra, three trusting children, were unaware of the enormous dangers they were about to face.

Judith

After Kristallnacht, my aunts and grandmother Grofa phoned each other continuously, trying to find a way of getting the three of us out of the country along with Hans Kroch's children. Whereas Hans Kroch's children had passports, which enabled them to leave Germany without any problems, for us three girls, things were different. We had to get out illegally; we had to be smuggled across the border.

Grofa realized that such a plan might be dangerous and did not want to make a decision without the consent of her daughter. But our mother was in the hospital with a nervous breakdown, being treated with sedatives that left her more asleep than awake. Nevertheless, she did understand that this was the only way her children could be saved and gave her consent. We were driven to the station in great secrecy because nobody was to notice that the Kroch children were leaving.

We said goodbye to Grofa and climbed into the train to Aachen without having said goodbye to Mutti, our mother.

This trip remains very clear in my memory. A chubby woman, a stranger, was responsible for the Kroch children, yet we felt quite alone. I dozed off a little from time to time but would wake up almost immediately because my heart was so heavy. The compartment was overheated, and the windows were shut. The rhythmic clanking of the wheels on the track did not let me rest. Every now and then I could see a light through the curtain as the train clattered on. We were going farther and farther away from everything we were used to, away from our safe home. Even when bad things were happening in the streets, our home had seemed to us peaceful and comforting.

From time to time, the train stopped at a station. I would pull the curtain aside and press my nose against the cold windowpane. The platforms were poorly illuminated and almost deserted. A few travelers would get on or off the train. The steam locomotive puffed and hissed. It was desolate. I was without Mutti for the first time.

The stationmaster whistled. Doors slammed shut. As the train began to move, it seemed as if the carriages were expanding. They squeaked a little until they became used to the increasing speed. I listened to the thrumming of the wheels interrupted by occasional drumbeats as we were crossing shunting points. Perhaps I dozed but did not sleep. I was miserable without Mutti. We left the train at Aachen, the last German city before Belgium.

Alexandra

The chubby woman then drove us in a car until we were out of town and told us, "Now you are close to the Belgian border, and you just walk down this road, and things will take care of themselves. It's all arranged. You just walk across the border. If you go straight here, you'll be all right."

So Eva and Judith and I were in the middle of nowhere on our own. It was farmland. We started walking. What else could we do? I was eleven, Judith was fourteen, and Eva was fifteen. I don't know how my older sisters felt. As long as I was with my older sisters, I had

31

some form of comfort. If I had been all by myself, I would have been really worried. I mean, I didn't feel very comfortable, but I didn't feel terribly worried, either. We each had a sandwich in our pocket, a cheese sandwich; nothing else. We had no money. We weren't supposed to have money. We walked for a fair amount of time. Then there was a fork in the road, and it was difficult to know which way to go. But my sisters made the decision to go that way, and so we went.

Judith

There was not a house or a soul to be seen anywhere around, only a red lane in the flat countryside that was broken by occasional hedges. The cold was bitter. We marched towards the horizon into the unknown. Suddenly a large German shepherd dog appeared before us and growled. We stood as if turned into stone and did not dare walk one step farther. Right behind the dog, a German border guard who must have been observing us from afar approached us. He asked us, not unkindly, who we were and where we came from. It must have been clear to him that he was talking to scared Jewish children. On the one hand we were afraid of the snarling dog; on the other we no longer felt so alone in the endless landscape and hoped that this man could help us. We had no idea how he could help us. We had not been told what was supposed to happen to us next, so that we would not inadvertently divulge the plan for our escape to Belgium. We told him our names and where we came from and that we wished to go to Belgium. The guard's main concern was whether we had any money with us. We did not have a penny.

The guard pointed in a certain direction and said, "That's where you have to go." We started to walk, hoping that we would soon be in Belgium. But after we had gone only a few steps the guard gave a command, and the big shepherd dog was at our heels, growling. We stopped, afraid. He called us back and interrogated us once more and then he let us go again. Yet even after our second attempt to follow his directions, he sent the well-trained dog to bring us back a third time. At that point the youngest, Alexandra, had had enough and started to cry. We were cold, hungry, and needed a bathroom. But most of all we were frightened.

Alexandra

Pretty soon we ran into the arms of a German border guard with a dog. He asked us what we were doing, who we were, and where we were going. We answered everything absolutely truthfully.

He said, "You can't just walk across the border. You have to come with me." And then he took us to the border guard house. This first soldier with the dog was fairly decent; he wasn't abusive, and he didn't make us feel bad.

He just told us, "I'm sorry, I can't let you go." Then at the border house, they were much meaner. There were two other soldiers there, and they asked us what we thought about Hitler because his picture was hanging there. We knew we had to be very careful about what we said. They asked, "Do you like him?"

And we replied, "Not very much." They didn't threaten us, but they made us feel uncomfortable.

Then they said, "Well, if you want to leave, you can't go to Belgium. We can't allow that. And where did you hide the money you were supposed to bring us?" We told them we had no money. So, one of them took us across the fields to a farmhouse where a farm woman stripped us bare of our clothes. She searched our bodies and our clothes and found a sandwich, opened the paper, took off the top layer, took off the cheese, and put it back together to see that we had hidden no money in the sandwich. Then she tapped the heels of our shoes to see if they were hollow, a hiding place for diamonds. She felt all the seams in our clothing and found nothing.

We were taken back to that border guard house, where we overheard the guards talk about what they were going to do with us now, because they weren't going to allow us to go to Belgium.

After a while, one of them announced to the others, "I'm going to take them back and show them the road back to Aachen, Germany."

He took us a fair way from the border house and said, "Well, now you go straight down that road and there are no more forks in the road, and you'll come to Aachen." So, we walked, and after a while, there were some crossroads.

Eva said to Judith, "If he says Aachen is that way, we should go the opposite direction."

Judith replied, "With that dog, if we don't do what he says, he'll have us back in a few minutes; and he can probably see us. We'd better do what he says and see what happens." So, we did that. I wasn't consulted. I was the baby.

Judith

He dropped us off at a lane that looked exactly like the last one, and maybe it was the same.

He commanded us, "Go!"

But I thought, "No, I want to go home. I don't want to walk along this same road anymore." We were worried that he might play the same games as the first guard with the German shepherd.

This uniformed man only repeated in a harsh tone, "Go! Go quickly in that direction." We were used to obeying adults and went off. The night was black, without moon or stars. We hardly saw the road in front of our feet and walked on without knowing where we were going. Our breath was freezing in our faces. There was no sound except that of our own steps on the solidly frozen ground. I just wanted to get away, far away, as quickly as possible.

Suddenly there were two soldiers standing before us. They shone their flashlights into our faces so that we could barely see them. Fright! A dreadful feeling of fright! What were we to do now? Eva, my older sister, could not go on. She turned around. She wanted to go back. She could not bear any more trouble from soldiers. I would have run as well, when a beam from their flashlights fell on one of their uniforms, illuminating a button on which I recognized a standing lion.

I called out, "Eva, Eva, the lion on the button! Don't run back to Germany. We are in Belgium!" This incident shows how worthwhile it can be to collect stamps, for in this instance my hobby probably saved our lives. I had recognized from seeing it on stamps, that the lion was the emblem of Belgium.

First, they took us to the guardroom. We sat by a large stove, where we thawed out and rested, believing ourselves safe. But it turned out differently. Since the Kristallnacht, hundreds of Jews were fleeing daily and illegally across the Belgian border. Germany's neighboring countries did not want to admit more refugees, so they sent them back.

Alexandra

In the guardroom, we were very nicely received by a lot of policemen who were sitting around the stove. They immediately offered us hot wine. That was the first time I drank undiluted wine. They wanted us to warm up. After a while the chief came. He was a jolly guy, and very apologetic, but he said he had to send us back to Germany. He had no authority to keep us because we had no visas. We had told him who we were. We hadn't lied at all. He explained that they were going to wait until it was the middle of the night, and then they were going to give us some guides and send us back where the German border guards would not find us.

We were sitting there having a relatively good time, when entered a couple, who seemed to be out of a movie. They were terribly tall and slender, and gorgeously dressed. The woman looked to me like the famous actress Marlene Dietrich. They went into the private office of the police chief and talked with him. When they came out, the police chief told us that these people were taking us back to Germany. We had no choice but to go with them.

Outside the police station, Eva confronted them, "Who are you? I want to know before I get into your car."

The woman said, "We are sent by your Uncle Marcel and Aunt Grete from Brussels, and we are taking you to them. We just told the Belgian police that we'd take you to Germany, but we are really taking you to Brussels."

Eva wanted proof. "How can I believe that you are going to do that?"

They laughed, and said, "Marcel told us that Eva would never go with us if we didn't have some proof." They showed us a picture of Marcel and Grete.

We did get in the car with them. We drove for a long way.

Then they told us, "Now we have to go back to the police station with an empty car to prove that we took you back to Germany.

So, you have to wait for us here." They put a blanket on the ground near a hedgerow next to an open field.

"Sit here and wait for us" they instructed. "We are going back to show the Belgian police our empty car. Then we will come back and pick you up and take you to Marcel and Grete."

Judith

So, there we were, three girls aged fifteen, fourteen, and eleven, dressed in hand tailored blue winter coats with velvet collars and matching hats. We were terribly afraid and miserable and not allowed to talk. An icy wind whistled fiercely around our ears. We waited, trembling in the dark night. The events of the day had been too upsetting. If we had been set down on the moon, it could not have seemed more bizarre to us.

I didn't know the exact plans for our escape, but from what I could piece together, an illegal Belgian organization had sent the chubby lady to Germany to bring us to the border, where the little girls without documents were sure to be detained. The German soldier who pretended to send us back to Leipzig was very likely a member of the same group. That is why he showed us the way to Belgium. Then he returned to the border post, probably claiming that he had dropped us off in Aachen.

The same ploy was used in Belgium. It was well known that the authorities no longer admitted refugees into Belgium. That is why Prince Charming and his Princess, the beautiful couple, were enlisted to appear on the Belgian side and to pretend to take us back to the German border guards. After a suitable interval, the pair returned to the Belgian post to announce that the girls had been driven back to Germany.

I cannot tell for how long we sat there, shivering in that field. Years! It was probably an hour or two. Meanwhile we suffered minute by minute; unhappy, cold, bewildered, and sick with longing for our mother.

Alexandra

We sat in the pitch-dark night, waiting. Time didn't go very fast, and we couldn't look at our watches; it was too dark. We just sat and waited, becoming quite uneasy by that time. We watched headlights come along the road. There weren't many cars. Once in a while, we noticed that there was a light coming by, and after a while we figured out that it was probably a searchlight from the border that came around very slowly.

Eva

Suddenly the beautiful couple was back, and with them a man named "Sonntag." He was apparently the person in charge. We were totally confused by the contrast. We had been huddled together for warmth by the hedge, and every time a vehicle passed by, we had pressed ourselves against the bushes and turned our faces away because we were afraid we might be seen. Now we were sitting in the backseat of a warm car.

After a while, we found ourselves in a very elegant restaurant in Liege. It was the first time I'd ever seen such a place, where you pay when you go in and then can eat anything you like. We looked elegant, too, in our fashionable winter clothes that had been made for us and fitted well. Though we had had a strange and exhausting day, I was not traumatized and had a healthy appetite. Little carts with the most wonderful food were wheeled past us, and I ate and ate. The climax was a dame blanche: vanilla ice-cream with a hot chocolate sauce and whipped cream. Our "saviors" had been paid well and let us eat to our heart's content.

Then we got in the car again, but then something curious happened. As the handsome man started the car, Mr. Sonntag suddenly stood in front of it, brightly illuminated by the headlights and shouted, "You are not moving from here!" A loud, furious quarrel ensued, a quarrel over money. Apparently, Marcel, our uncle, had paid the couple, and they didn't want to give Sonntag his share. They simply began to drive and almost ran him over. Somebody pulled him away, and there we left him shouting and waving his arms.

Alexandra

We drove on, and I fell asleep. When we arrived in Brussels, we expected to meet Aunt Grete, Uncle Marcel, and their son Martin. But our drivers informed us that they couldn't bring us to our aunt and uncle at this hour of the morning. By that time, it was in the predawn hours. They told us that later in the morning, Marcel and Grete would come and pick us up. They were both obviously artists, which is why Marcel and Grete knew them, because they were artists, too. We slept in their studio on a very soft bed with lots of pillows.

Eva

On the ground lay a wonderful Afghan hound with long hair, elegantly eccentric; a long, high-backed animal with floppy ears. Next to him was a big easel on which stood a picture by El Greco. Whether it was genuine or not, I could not judge. The three of us slept very well in a large bed, and in the early morning we came down to have breakfast. It was very pleasant. Suddenly we heard the front doorbell ring violently and heard the voice of Uncle Marcel screaming furiously at this couple. They shouted back as Marcel forced his way in, pulled us to the door, pushed us into his car and sped away.

Uncle Marcel was quite pale and breathless and said, "Thank God I managed to get hold of you!" He'd found out that these people dealt in white slavery. They sold young girls. Mr. Sonntag had probably been the one to tell him. Mr. Sonntag most likely dealt in young girls himself, but his anger against the "beautiful couple" made him take his revenge.

After a day or two in my uncle and aunt's house, we were sent to another part of Brussels to stay with two old widowers whose family name was Geis. These two old gentlemen, who had no children, had agreed to take three girls into their home. A few weeks later, we left the brothers Geis and stayed at a children's home for girls in Westende by the North Sea.

It was here that I experienced something that made me afraid of the North Sea for the rest of my life. At low tide, the water recedes very far. When the tide returns, the water comes back like a wall. In order to get down to the beach, we had to descend about 30 steps. The stairs were positioned along the shore at regular intervals every twenty meters. On this particular day I went for a walk along the beach with Judith. The water was far away, and we did not know that the tide had turned, and therefore did not expect the water to come so fast. Suddenly we saw this ten-meter-high wall of water racing towards us like millions of trampling horses. We were between two sets of stairs and ran like mad, absolutely terrified. We got to the stairs and ran up as fast as we could. We reached the top with our last strength and threw ourselves on the ground to catch our breath. If we had not noticed the tide coming in when we did, it is possible that on the next day they would have found two drowned girls.

Judith

We lived from day to day. We did not know who from our family would retrieve us, or when they would come. I didn't think of bad things. I did not imagine that something terrible could happen. I had the feeling that my parents were here with me, and that I was not alone.

One day, after having spent about three months in Belgium, our Papa arrived and took us to France to be reunited with our mother and brother. We were more than happy.

Papa Fritz said, "Now everything will be all right. We never have to see the Germans again." My father was no clairvoyant.

Much later we heard what had happened to our mother. While we were walking through the countryside to Belgium, she was lying sedated, in the hospital. Grofa was notified of our arrival in Belgium that very night. She immediately phoned the hospital and asked that my mother be told her children were safe. The nurse on night duty hurried to Mutti's bed and gave her the good tidings.

Mutti said, "Thank you" and went back to sleep. Suddenly she awoke in total terror. She could remember only that her children were on a dangerous journey to Belgium and was full of fear because she had not yet heard from them. She was tortured by the most dreadful thoughts but did not dare to ask if there had been a message for her.

At last, the nurse came back to her bed and said in a friendly voice, "Good morning, Frau Kroch. Didn't I bring you good news during the night?"

Mutti recovered within a few weeks, so that at the beginning of 1939 she was able to escape to Switzerland with the help of a paid smuggler. The Rhine River forms a border between Germany and Switzerland, and the smuggler found a place where the Rhine was dry. Our mother had to crawl on her stomach across the dry tributary of the Rhine. When she was on the other side of the Rhine, she was in Switzerland, and there she had family, who took her in. Papa Fritz went to Switzerland to fetch Mutti and brought her to France, where she was reunited with Peter, who had escaped from Germany.

Alexandra

Our brother, Peter, had gotten out of Leipzig in the following way. Uncle Curt's youngest child, Henry, was in a school in Switzerland and had returned home to Germany for his vacation. Shortly before the Germans did all the arresting of the Polish Jews, the school sent word to all their Jewish students from Germany. "You'd better come back to Switzerland before the vacation is over if you want to come back at all."

When Henry heard this, he told my parents, "We've got to get Peter out." Peter was not at all involved with that school, but he had the same last name as his cousin. So, Peter and Henry went to the border between Germany and Switzerland, where they stood on the German side with the other students returning to school. A school representative read from a list of legitimate students enrolled in that school. The Germans would send the particular student with that name over to the Swiss authorities, where they would stand on the Swiss side of the border until everyone was called.

When they called, "Kroch," Peter (instead of Henry) crossed over to the Swiss side. Very quickly, Peter said he needed to go to the bathroom and disappeared. This was all prearranged. When the list was read and finished, Henry Kroch was still standing on the German side.

The person in charge asked, "Who are you?"

He explained, "I'm Henry Kroch."

The man replied, "But we checked you off."

So, Henry answered, "Well, I don't know who you checked off, but I'm Henry Kroch." He showed them his papers, which were in order. There was no question that he was who he was, and his teachers from the other side of the border line confirmed, "Yes, that's our student." And that's how Peter got out. We had lots of family in Switzerland. He just disappeared and went to our relatives in Switzerland, and eventually joined us in Paris.

Judith

At first, we lived in Paris near the Gare Montparnasse at the Hotel du Commerce. This small hotel had a spiral staircase that led to little rooms used by passing couples. At the end of the short hallway was a toilet for each floor. The bathroom was always locked: one could take a bath only by permission from the landlady after paying a fee. In a nearby street there was a kosher pension where we ate our meals and spent the High Holidays.

The Krochs' standard of living had gone down considerably, yet we were cheerful and glad to be together. After a while our shrinking capital forced us to move out of the expensive city of Paris into a house in Chaville, just outside of Paris. The move was made more urgent by the arrival of our Grofa, who had obtained a visa for France and had left Germany legally. Under no circumstances could she have been expected to live in a hotel with a spiral staircase and prostitutes.

Grofa was a fearless woman. As a young girl she had been invited to climb into one of the first automobiles, a vehicle without a roof. Now she had boarded a plane in order to avoid a long and tiring journey by train. Civil aviation flourished only after the Second World War. Before this, flying was a great adventure. There was no separate cabin for the pilot. He sat in the front like a bus driver and steered his plane through the wind. Later we learned that Grofa was on the last flight out of Germany before the war broke out.

Chapter Five
France, 1939-1940

The Kroch family was reunited in France without a minute to spare. On Friday, September 1, 1939, Germany invaded Poland, and two days later France declared war on Germany. Though five million Frenchmen were mobilized to serve in the army, they actually never engaged in battle of any kind for eight months; thus, this action was deemed a "drole guerre" (phony war).[6]

The complacency of the French army was due to the misguided perception that the country was protected from German invasion because they had built the Maginot Line. This fortified barrier, consisting of concrete and weapons, stretched for two hundred eighty miles along the border between France and its neighbors, Germany, Switzerland and Luxembourg. Ultimately, this blockade did nothing to deter the German army, which marched through the unprotected border of Belgium into France on May 10, 1940. France accepted defeat on June 14.

During this time, General Petain was appointed prime minister of France. His headquarters were in Vichy, France. On June 22, Petain signed an armistice, which decreed that France be divided into a Northern Zone, under German occupation, and a Southern Free Zone, which was to continue to be governed by the French. Paris was in the Occupied Zone. Article 19 of the armistice stipulated that the French hand over any German Jewish refugees requested by the Third Reich. Thus, the first step towards deportations was put into place.[7] Eventually all Jews living in France were slated for deportation, no matter where they resided, or whether they were foreign born, or French naturalized citizen.

The Kroch family had fled Germany hoping to find a safe haven in France. As history unfolded, the family came to realize how wrong they were. The Krochs were not alone. Estimates suggest that there were forty thousand Jews who had immigrated to France from the Third Reich.[8]

During October of 1940, Petain unveiled the first of many

edicts called the "Statut des Juifs," which eventually became the law throughout the unoccupied and occupied zones. These antisemitic laws were to gradually and firmly dismantle the civil rights of the Jews and expose them to increasing hostility and aggression from the French. In his zeal to impress the Nazis, Petain had implemented laws that were more stringently antisemitic than those proposed by the German occupiers. One after another the proclamations rolled out, eerily mimicking those that had been enacted by the Third Reich in Germany. Jews were forced to register, required to have a "J" written on their identity papers, prohibited from working in public service, lost their rights to practice their professions, and eventually were required to give up their businesses, possessions, and property. [9]

Gradually the French Jews not only realized that the Vichy regime was not going to protect them, but in fact it became increasingly clear that the Vichy was a puppet of the Nazi regime, only too willing to do its bidding. And, with great similarity to the German Jews, the assimilated French-born Jews reacted at first with the same degree of naivety, convincing themselves that their allegiance to their country would protect them from antisemitic laws. The Krochs, as was the case with many other Jewish immigrants in France, were more aware of the fate that could befall them, since they had already witnessed the violence perpetrated on them by the Nazis in their German homeland.

Despite their vigilance and planning, the Kroch family met with unexpected, life threatening setbacks at every turn.

Eva

We first rented a house in Chaville for the summer, because the owners had gone away on vacation. When the family returned, we moved to a tiny house next door that was the summer house of a concierge who had moved back to Paris at the end of the summer. It was built like a triangle, with two long walls, and one short one facing the street that was just over a meter wide and contained the front door. At the back it was about five meters wide, and behind it were planted beans and other vegetables. In the left pointed part was a bedroom, then a living room and kitchen, and then another long, narrow bedroom.

For two women and a child it was ideal, but we were seven people. My parents slept in the one bed, Grofa and I slept in a big bed in the narrow room, and in the living room were Judith, Alexandra, and Peter on folding beds.

It was here that I learned French. In the living room was a small, glass-fronted cupboard containing at least 100 cheap romance novels: "The poor girl who came to town from the country and how the poor girl became happy and how the poor girl became unhappy." I cried as I read through the books, and by the time I was imprisoned in the Gurs internment camp, I spoke the language fluently.

Judith

Alexandra and I attended the Ecole Communale in Chaville. How different it was from the Carlebach School in Leipzig! Here the children could romp around freely on the playground, where we danced and played games and – oh, miracle – we could participate even though we were Jewish. I was overwhelmed by such kindness. Boys and girls were taught in separate buildings, and the playground was divided by a high wall. Everyone wore an apron wrapped over their clothes: boys and girls alike. Alexandra and I studied hard and with pleasure. For the first time in my life, I became a good student.

Alexandra

The school in Chaville is where I had the best teacher that was ever created, called Mme. Mille. In this sixth-grade class were fifty-five children, some of whom had been held back three times – because in France you could not go to the next grade if you didn't pass the exam. There were some kids who were old enough to leave school by law, but their parents didn't want them out of school, so they remained. On the other hand, you could also skip a grade. Eleven was the average age, and there were also fifteen-year-old students. So, it was a very difficult class to teach.

Mme. Mille had a system which by American standards would

be totally outlawed. She taught to the best students. We were ranked by our grades every two weeks. She seated us with the best student right in front of her desk and the worst student as far away from her as possible, way in back in the opposite corner. The ranking snaked back and forth that way, so that all good students were close by the blackboard and by her.

When she seated us after the ranking, she would always say, "Anybody who wants to work and wants to answer questions, raise your hand, I will call on you. If you don't want to participate, all I'm asking of you is to be quiet. I am not forcing you to do anything, but if you want to work, I will work with you, and then you will come forward."

Every morning started with dictation. Three or four girls would stand at the blackboard, among them a very good one: never any of the really bad students from the back row. Mme. Mille would correct the best answer on the blackboard.

After everybody had made their corrections, she would ask, "Who had no mistakes, raise your hand. Who had two mistakes? Who had four mistakes?" And so on. She would compliment those who made progress, but not comment too much on the ones who had more than twenty mistakes. In my first dictation, I think I had thirty-seven mistakes in about six lines. I erased, and then did the next one, erased, and the next one. I learned very quickly that way. There was no pressure. It wasn't graded.

In addition to working in school, she did something that no other teacher I know would ever do. On Thursday mornings (we had no school on Thursdays), she invited every one of us to come to her house and work with her. There were usually between six and twelve girls from the class, including me, who would turn up at her house. The dining table was something that would be worth a mint today, a very dark, huge, oak dining table with twelve chairs around it. We would sit around the table working on the exercises she assigned us. Mme. Mille sat nearby in an armchair, knitting and correcting our work. I spent from nine o'clock to noon every Thursday morning studying with Mme. Mille, no charge. And since I wanted to do well, I took advantage of it, and I did very well. It was probably my best time in school. I learned French mostly from her. When I started, I could barely speak

French, and I certainly couldn't read and write it properly.

At the end of the year was the Certificat D'Etude. We all worked for that diploma because that was officially the end of obligatory schooling, at age twelve. However, the war wanted otherwise, because we couldn't finish; we couldn't get the Certificat D'Etude then. We had to postpone it because of various air raids. But I did eventually get it.

Eva

I attended a strict Catholic school in Paris for a year. The morning began with a prayer sung in Latin:

"O cor amoris victim,
Celi pereme gaudium
Mortalium solatiuum
Mortalium spes ultima."

I didn't understand the words and wasn't forced to participate. The teachers told me to stand there like everyone else but reassured me that I did not have to pray. All schools in France had a uniform, and we wore a light beige apron with long sleeves with a square collar and fine white edging around the collar and the cuffs of the long sleeves. And, of course, we wore stockings, a hat and gloves. On the way from my house to the school and back, I had to wear the uniform. After school I could wear what I liked, and it did not matter if a teacher saw me with bare legs and sandals. Teachers and pupils were very nice to me. The fact that my father sent me to this school was proof of his tolerance. He didn't think that attending a Catholic school would turn me into a Catholic. The people who ran the school were pleasant and nice, and I enjoyed being there.

I had to go home in the dark. The way led through a tree-lined avenue that was unlit because of the war. One evening, under these trees, I was attacked by two men. I begged them to leave me in peace, but they only laughed.

So, I said, "You can hear by my accent that I am not French. If somebody sees you with me, you can be taken to a war tribunal." So, they vanished.

Judith

Following the German invasion of Poland, the United Kingdom and France declared war on Germany, and the war in the West began. We were waiting in Chaville, rather perplexed, to see what would happen. There was no fear yet. Gas masks were distributed, and we had to carry them around with us. Then the sirens began to wail their enemy aircraft warnings.

In 1939, there were no rockets yet. They were developed later, aimed at England. Airplanes were sighted when they crossed from Germany over the French border. Paris had been declared an open city and was thus not supposed to be bombed. But we were living in Chaville, very close to the military airfield of Villacoublay, and we were therefore in a danger zone.

Alexandra

Chaville was between three airports, so there were many air raids, because airports were targets for the Germans. When we were at home and they sounded the alarm, the entire neighborhood went to the cellar of a nunnery. It was originally a wine cellar and had a vaulted ceiling. We stayed there until we heard the short bursts of the "all-clear" signal.

During school, we had two air raid drills a day. The older girls, like Judith, had to go to the rooms of the little girls (younger than me), and each big girl had to take the hands of two little girls and lead them in an orderly fashion down the road. My group was supposed to go by ourselves. The director, Mme. Helier, would sound the alarm and the all-clear with her whistle. She would never announce ahead of time when she would give an alarm. Nobody told us where we were going, and when we got to the corner, we stopped and went back to the school. Where we were headed if it were a real alarm, we were never told.

Then one day there was a real siren alarm while we were in school, and all hell broke loose. The big girls ran the fastest, and the little girls ran in circles and cried, and we stood there at a loss. We went to the corner and didn't know where to go next. We eventually found out that the air raid shelter was a deep, large mushroom-growing cave about a kilometer or two down the road, a long way away. There we waited until the all-clear signal came. The amusing thing was that all this practice did no good when the real air raid happened.

We had to go to school with a gas mask. The gas masks were handed out by the mayor's office, and everybody had a gas mask fitted. It was a rubbery type of face mask, with a cylinder through which you breathed. This gas mask was packed in a metal cylinder, which we wore over our shoulders or around our necks and was obligatory. If you forgot it, you had to go back home and get it before returning to school. And this led to a very fortuitous situation. If you didn't do your history homework, or hadn't read your science chapter, that was when you "remembered" that you "forgot" your mask. You couldn't use this excuse very often, but it worked quite nicely a few times. The cylinders all looked the same, so there had to be some way to tell them apart, and since the littlest girls couldn't read, we had to pick a symbol or character to identify our cylinder. Mine was a little piggy. Fortunately, we never had to use the gas masks.

Judith

Just as the German civilians had done in their country, the French citizens were also lulled into a stupid feeling of complacency. Had France not built the impregnable Maginot line? This was supposed to defend the French border. No one in the French General Command had foreseen, not even in their worst nightmares, that the Germans would, in a few days, simply march into Holland, through Belgium, and into France, leaving the "impregnable" Maginot line aside.

The small amount of money my father had brought with him was in German currency, and therefore no longer exchangeable. In short, we were left penniless. Papa had attempted to build up a business in Paris with the help of some friends, but the times were too uncertain, and his efforts were unsuccessful. We were forced to move out of our pretty home in Chaville into a tiny house in the backyard.

Although he never showed his concern, my father took certain measures that showed how circumspect he was. He called his wife, mother-in-law, and four children together and gave us several addresses of families abroad.

"Should we get separated by the war, we will always find each other again through these addresses," he reassured us. The meeting place in France was in Mézières-en-Brenne, a small village in the center of France where his friend Félix Goldschmidt had bought a house and taken his family of seven to wait out the war. The address lists were then wrapped in waterproof material and made into little packets, which we wore around our necks. Grofa was the only one to be angry with her son-in-law, Fritz. She felt that his precautions created an unnecessary sense of panic.

Home in Chaville

Chapter Six
Internment, 1939-1940

There was a short interval between the time that France declared war on Germany in September of 1939 until France accepted defeat in June 1940. During that period Petain's Vichy regime decided to intern all enemy aliens (or "undesirables," as they were called). There was no logic to the reasoning that these German Jewish emigrants would pose a threat. They were, in fact, refugees who had been prosecuted by the Third Reich, and therefore had reason to feel even more animosity towards the Germans than the typical French person.

During the fall and winter of 1939, all German Jewish males between the ages of seventeen and fifty-five, and all unmarried and childless women in that age group, who had immigrated to France were arrested as enemy aliens and sent to internment camps, which the French called "lodging centers." By the end of 1939, it is estimated that fifteen thousand Jews who had fled the Third Reich had been arrested.[10] Peter and Fritz Kroch were among those deemed a threat and sent to an internment camp. Later, when Eva turned seventeen, she was also considered a threat, and she, too, was sent to an internment camp.

Living conditions at the camps were primitive and appalling. Inmates were left unprotected from the harsh weather conditions of extreme heat or cold. The inhumane treatment of its prisoners was due not only to indifference by the French, but also from deliberate ill will.[11] Many thousands of Jews died in these camps. Gurs, where Eva was imprisoned, was one of the largest and well known camps, infamous for having some of the worst conditions.[12]

Peter and Fritz were imprisoned in a lesser known camp called Athis-de-l'Orne. Surprisingly, none of the girls describe the moments when their father and brother were arrested. Not so surprisingly, the two men did not share accounts of their experiences during their months at the camp. Both were very upbeat men who focused on the positive. Like many other Holocaust survivors, they buried their painful memories.

In the confusion of the fall of France, and for a few weeks following the armistice, many of the internees either escaped or were released by guards who were either indifferent or wanted to help them stay out of the Nazi hands. For a brief period in May and June, Gurs was abandoned and many women prisoners left on their own.[13] We also know that Peter and Fritz were released around the same time from different sections of Athis-de-l'Orne. Not knowing of the fate of the rest of the family, each made their way separately to the first address on the note hanging around their necks: Félix Goldschmidt's home in Mézières-en-Brenne.

Peter's only baggage was his precious violin, which he had inherited from his grandfather Rafael Frank, who, in his youth, had bought it from a widow for little money because it was in poor condition. While it was being repaired, it became evident that this instrument dated back to the sixteenth or seventeenth century and was crafted by a family of violin builders named Amati, the Rolls-Royce of violins.

Shortly after the abrupt closing of the internment camps, they were reopened and used as holding facilities prior to deportation to concentration camps. Drancy was the largest camp, with the worst conditions. Roughly sixty-seven thousand Jews were interned there and later deported to concentration camps. Less than three percent survived.

Eva's description of her imprisonment at age seventeen is remarkable. Her optimistic spirit and her active imagination allowed Eva to transcend the brutal realities, and to paint a picture of resiliency and hope.

Judith

Twice a week we had to report to the Chaville police station as enemy aliens. We became good friends with the gendarmes. The French authorities, however, became concerned about the possibility of having "German spies" in their midst. They had the "brilliant" idea of arresting and interning all German-Jewish refugees of a certain age. Most likely the real German spies were going about their business with false papers. Because the authorities worried that Papa Fritz and Peter could be German spies, they were taken to an internment camp in the

51

north-western part of the country called Athis-de-l'Orne. They took Eva, too, because they thought that certainly she must be a cunning German secret agent. She was interned in Gurs, in the Pyrenees, as soon as she turned seventeen.

And our good old Grofa; she was "really dangerous." She was picked up some time later in such a state of shock that she got diarrhea, and the agents who had come to get her had to wait for a considerable time. Forty-eight hours later, Grofa was sent back home. They knew how to deal with spies, but not with diarrhea.

Eva

Six months after war was declared, I turned seventeen. My father and Peter had both been taken to a French internment camp as "enemy Germans," and now I suddenly belonged to the age group in which women, too, were interned. I was the only one of the female members of our family who had to go. Grofa was too old, and Mutti had young children. I remember that I was nevertheless pleased with the idea of being seventeen years old.

First my mother went to the police with me and asked if it was really necessary for a seventeen-year-old girl to go to a camp, and the police officer told her, "There's nothing we can do. It's a law. She has to go, and if she doesn't, we'll have to fetch her and put her in prison."

I have a peculiar nature. It has always been this way. If something cannot be changed, I look for something positive. I think this is on the whole a good thing. I got this from my father. He was the optimist. He was always sure of everything. I had the feeling that nothing could happen and that it would end well. So, I felt that having to go to a camp was very interesting. My mother accompanied me to Montfort L'Amaury by train, and then I was left alone. This was a private house that was the first stop before being sent to Gurs, the internment camp. My first impression was wonderful; the gate, the whole entrance was covered by a vine full of light violet flowers that hung in clusters like bunches of grapes. But I suppose I must also have been very agitated.

When I came to the room to which I was assigned, there was a girl, about my age, with her mother, both also bound for Gurs. The room we occupied was on the first floor of a very old villa. The girl slept between her mother and me. There was no work for us to do except keep our rooms clean. The girl and her mother lay on their beds while I did the cleaning. When an officer came to the door, the mother took me by the arm, and we went for a walk. When we came back, the girl had butter and meat and all sorts of other food. Some of it she gave to me in exchange for the cleaning I did. I was glad we had this arrangement because I enjoyed the extra food. I had absolutely no idea what it all meant.

It wasn't so bad there. But after two days, someone came into the room and informed us that we'd be leaving for Gurs the next morning. It turned out to be a train journey of three days and two nights. In normal times it would have taken twelve or fifteen hours, but the train was slow and sometimes was shunted to a railway siding and stood stationary for hours. The train was so packed that many people had to stand. Luckily for us, we had succeeded in getting places to sit. But sitting for two to three days is also not easy. The mother, the girl, and I looked after each other's places if one of us had to get up. We were not given anything to eat during those three days and ate only what we had brought with us. I had a few tins of sardines. Everybody had something, and we all shared.

We finally arrived in Gurs. This was a huge camp at the foot of the Pyrenees. The area is called the desert of France. There were no trees; nothing but glaring sun. The nearest city is Lourdes, where believing Catholics went to be cured of their ailments. Gurs had been established for Spaniards who had fled Spain during their Civil War. They could not go back to Franco, and France did not want them. Gurs was staffed by French soldiers who supervised the prisoners, and also by Spaniards who did the menial work. It housed thousands of inmates. Gurs camp was divided into îlots (little islands). Each îlot held 60 barracks standing side by side and back to back, and each was surrounded by barbed wire. In one direction the îlots stretched in a straight line, and in the other they were bordered by broad streets of packed dry sand in the summer, and mud in the winter; wide enough for three traffic lanes, which divided one long line of îlots from the other. One could walk for twenty minutes and see nothing but barbed wire fencing, behind which stood long lines of barracks divided into îlots. Every îlot was identified by a letter of the alphabet, and mine was "I." Opposite my îlot and divided from us by two barbed wire fences and a broad street was îlot "J." This is important to know because of what happened later.

I was not together with the mother and daughter anymore, but soon found other people to talk to. The women were mostly very nice, and one in particular was overly protective since I was, after all, only seventeen, and the youngest in the barrack. It was only June when I got there, but the heat was dreadful. The barracks were made of wood with small windows. There was not a breath of air. People lay on their mattresses and boiled. We were thirty women on each side, with just enough room between the mattresses to put our feet down. On each straw mattress was a blanket, and both the mattress and the blanket were covered with stains and dirt.

Luckily, I found a way of being a little cooler. The barrack roofs almost reached the ground on either side, and I was so thin that I managed to push myself under the roof down to the side of the wall and in this way had some shade. There I was alone because people of normal proportions could not squeeze themselves in there. The sunlight was blinding day after day. It never rained. The heat was reflected by the light-colored sand, and the air trembled. When I went inside, it took time for my eyes to adjust. And then I saw long lines of mattresses, and on them lay women sleeping, sighing and sometimes weeping.

Outside, the Spaniards cleaned and swept the îlots, row by row, along endless fences. One young woman in my barrack would talk to these workers, and I liked standing there with her, until the overprotective woman who slept near me pulled me away and told me to have nothing to do with her.

We each had a plate and a spoon. We would stand outside when it was time for lunch, and the kitchen would bring out a big tub of soup, which consisted of water with some vegetables floating in it. We also got oxtail (bones with tough meat), or not quite cooked fish. I had good teeth and a healthy stomach. The poor women who could not eat and digest this food ate only the absolute minimum and gave the rest to me. So, I was never hungry. I did not eat kosher food anymore. I still had a tiny bit of money, so with this I bought a small piece of butter every week and had some fat in my diet.

I would walk through the camp in all directions and watch the people and observe everything else happening around me. I found things that were good: fascinating people, women with beautiful hair, and I had some interesting conversations. There were also things that were not at all nice, for instance, the toilets. They were in a wooden structure on stilts that were well anchored to the ground, to which we had to climb up six or seven steps. The floor inside was made of wooden planks with round holes cut out at regular intervals. Between the holes were wooden walls, and each had a door. There one squatted, and if one wished to see one's neighbor, one could do so. Under the holes were huge, deep containers. Spaniards came and lifted the containers with big, heavy iron bars and deposited them on a special train. Empty containers were then positioned in each latrine.

One day when I was crouching there busy with my own affairs, a woman came in next to me, and I suddenly heard her swear, "Damn it, just when I'd learned how to aim straight, and now I have to learn to aim sideways," referring to the new position of the container under her. That was funny. But on another occasion a woman took out her false teeth for some reason and accidentally dropped them into the hole. It was almost a death sentence for her because how would she be able to chew on the tough meat and fish? She screamed, and a woman on her other side came over to see if she could help. As the helper looked down, her glasses fell into the hole. This may sound a bit funny, but it was tragic.

Another day I heard that the Germans had killed all the Jews in Athis, and I feared that my father was among them. A few days later as I was walking around the barracks passing the time, I heard two women talking.

One of them said, "My husband was in Athis, and your husband was there, too, wasn't he? I heard that a number of the camp inmates managed to escape from the massacre and go to Albi."

I approached these two women and said, "If you don't mind, I would like to pay for a third of a postcard to Albi to find if my father, who was in Athis, too, was among those that got away." In this way I found out that my father was alive. However, I knew nothing about the rest of the family.

When people received letters, the authorities called out your name, and you went to a small hut some îlots away where they passed them out. My letters were addressed: Eva Kroch, Îlot I, Gurs, Basses, Pyrénées. One day I heard them call out, "Cecile Lande." Cecile (or Cilla as we called her) was Mutti's cousin.

So, I went to the gate and explained to the guard, "There was no post for me today, but I just heard them call out my cousin's name. I didn't know she was here, and if you allow me to go to the post hut, I'll find her." So, he allowed me to go. Cilla suggested that I come to her barrack in Îlot J. I received permission because there were some free beds there. And so, I marched across the street with my suitcase.

Occasionally, a list was circulated by the camp management, and you put your name on the list if the circumstance related to you, and then hoped that you would be freed. One list you signed if you had a stomach ulcer, and another list you signed if you had young children dependent on you. You signed another list if you came from the southern free zone. Cilla and I signed this list because her father, my Great Uncle Wilhelm, lived in Avignon, which was in the free zone. It was a lie since I didn't live there.

A few days later, somebody came into the barrack and said, "Miss Kroch, come! You, and you, and you: come," and then pointed at a few women, but not at Cilla.

She cried, "What about me?"

And the man replied, "No, not you." I was freed and she was not. She had to stay there another month or two, and it was terrible for her because she was not a healthy person. She was bitterly hurt by this, and never truly forgave me. I can't really blame her. I had signed my name on the list with a lie, and she had to suffer for it. If it hadn't been for me, she might have been back with her parents earlier.

In Avignon I found Uncle Wilhelm, my grandmother Grofa's brother-in-law, and his wife (Grofa's sister), Tante Ida. On my very first day there, I went to the Red Cross and made some inquiries about my brother, but they didn't know anything about Peter.

My Uncle Wilhelm employed a woman who washed his feet and went for walks with him. His wife had to stay at home or walk three steps behind him. I know from my grandmother that in earlier days he sometimes locked up his wife, Ida. He was such a philanderer that he assumed that she might behave like him.

During the day, I stayed with Uncle Wilhelm and Tante Ida, and at night I slept at the Grillon Hotel, where I shared a room with the Hungarian woman who washed his feet. Ms. Farago gave me her 12-year-old son's bed, and he slept in the other bed with her. She was alone with her son because she had sent her husband to war.

Being a Hungarian citizen, she thought it wise to tell him, "Be a French soldier, join the army, and when the war is over, we will have French papers and will be much better off." Of course, she never thought he would be killed. He lost his life somewhere in the Somme, one of the unknown soldiers who never returned. She never forgave herself. The son played the violin beautifully and spoke French with a perfect Marseilles accent. Both were killed by the Germans.

The elevator in the Grillon Hotel was old. When one pressed the button on the outside, it went up or down accordingly. However, it did not respond to the wishes of the passengers inside. Sometimes the concierge and I would take the German officers who were also guests of the hotel on involuntary rides. I stood on the ground floor and would press the elevator to the fourth floor, and he would stand on the fourth floor and press the button back down to the ground floor.

One day I was in the hotel room in Avignon and was called to the lobby. I thought the Germans had found out that I was taking them on elevator rides. The sun was dazzlingly bright outside, and the inside of the hotel was dark.

Two very tall men who looked German came in speaking French, and one said, "Are you Eva Kroch?" using the familiar "Tu." I thought he was going to beat me.

I said, "Yes." He replied, "Je suis Peter," "I am Peter."

And I said, "Why are you making fun of me? I don't know where my brother is, and I don't know you!"

So, he came up to me very close and said, "Look at me. I am your brother!" I wept with joy.

Peter had been in the internment camp together with the second tall man and had been released when the Germans took over the camp.

He decided not to go to Mézières, but instead he wanted to join an army in Algeria to fight against the Germans. In Bordeaux, many people tried to go to Algeria by boat. Three ships were to leave. The first was torpedoed and sank with all the passengers. The second was also hit and limped back to harbor. Peter was going to board the third boat, but upon seeing what happened to the other two boats, he made the decision to remain behind. Instead of leaving France, he made his way to reunite with our family in Mézières.

He travelled on foot with his friend, living in dread of being caught by either the Germans or the French militia, since he had no papers. On their way they met Rabbi Ochs, who had been in the first camp with my father and Peter and knew them both. The rabbi knew where my father was, and Peter got in touch with him. That is how Peter found out that I was in Avignon with Uncle Wilhelm, because my father had received this information. So, Peter, my father, and I were in touch. But my mother, sisters, and Grofa had vanished.

One morning I was having breakfast with my Uncle Wilhelm and Aunt Ida when a pre-printed postcard arrived. "I am well, ill, happy" (circle the correct response). So and so is at this place: _____ Signed by _____." This was the only way that people could communicate by post, and it probably served the Germans well. On this postcard, a certain Laura had written that she, Jeanne, Julie, and Frieda were well and at a certain place. She asked for information about Peter, Helene, and Frederic. Aunt Ida could not make heads or tails of the postcard and thought that it was all a mistake, until I explained that Laura was Lenore, our mother. Jeanne was Johanna, our grandmother. Julie was Judith, and Frieda was Alexandra. She wanted information about Peter, Helene (this was my second name) and Frederic (her husband, Fritz). I immediately wrote back to her, using the same names. And so, I was really the one who by chance got the family in touch with each other again.

View of the Gurs Transit Camp from the water tower
Courtesy of the United States Holocaust Memorial Museum

Chapter Seven
Félix Goldschmidt

Félix and Fritz had known each other in Leipzig Germany; however, they did not become friends until 1939 when they reconnected in Paris. It was there that Félix invited Fritz and his family to join him in Mézières-en-Brenne should the Kroch family need a place to keep a low profile. Félix was to become my grandfather's best friend. They had a lot in common. Both fought in WW1 for Germany and both were observant Jews. It was, however, their similar personalities that created such a powerful bond. They shared a characteristic that was quite unique. Each took himself very lightly, enjoying banters that could well have been considered very silly and childish. They came up with bathroom humor jingles, made funny sounds and delighted each other with impromptu antics.

Félix had chosen the small village of Mézières-en-Brenne in southern France as a safe home for his wife and five children because it was not strategically important militarily to either side, and because it was in the middle of nowhere. Later, he would discover how sympathetic the villagers, the police and the Mayor of Mézières were to its Jewish families.

Peter, Fritz, and Eva were on their own and each knew that they had to find a way to Félix Goldschmidt. Lore, Grofa, Judith, and Alexandra were together and had to find a way to get there as well. They all knew that their family strength and their survival rested on their unity. Félix had offered them a safe haven. Now they needed luck and determination to reach him.

Félix Goldschmidt was a heroic man who saved not only the Kroch family. Estimates are that he saved between 200 and 300 Jews. Goldschmidt, as he was lovingly called, worked for the resistance movement in many capacities. In addition to forging fake identity papers, he also assembled explosives for the underground and funneled bribes to free prisoners. He had given instructions to his wife and children that if he were to be arrested, they should immediately gather all the fake identity papers that were at their home and throw them into the cesspool behind their house.

Félix risked his life many times. Yet he knew well that if he were to be apprehended, he would not be able to rely on the help of others. Being arrested as a resistance fighter was quite simply a death sentence. And eventually when this happened, he needed to devise his own plan for escape.

Félix Goldschmidt

Fritz and Félix

Eva

My father was the first to arrive at his friend Félix Goldschmidt's home. Peter arrived next, and now it was my turn. I had decided to stay with Uncle Wilhelm and Aunt Ida until Cilla joined us. I set out on Friday, the 13th of September, 1940, since I knew that this was a lucky day for me. I went by train from Avignon to Chateauroux, and then changed to a slow country train as far as Buzançais. From there I met a man with a wagon who took me to Subtray, and here Peter picked me up with his friend René Klein, and we walked about one and a half kilometers to Goldschmidt's house. René had a small tin trumpet and sang all sorts of children's nonsense songs while we walked. My father and Félix came to meet us along the way, and so I was received by four nice gentlemen. Together we reached Les Vignes, a rundown farmhouse, Félix's castle.

The road to Les Vignes was unpaved, an old, sandy country track. The Goldschmidts' house had a large room downstairs consisting of a big kitchen, dining and living space. The kitchen area held a big cast-iron cooking stove with a metal canister built in on the side, where water was heated. In the corner was an old wash basin made of stone, and in the middle stood a huge, rectangular table with two long benches along each side, and an old, heavy chair at the end.

To get upstairs, one had to walk up an outside stairway that led upwards at a slant along the wall, and ended on a platform that continued as an open corridor along the front of the house. On the right was a very large room where Félix, his wife, and all five children slept. The other big room was on the left and was used for drying apples, pears and string beans. And here was where my father slept and later my mother, also, when she eventually arrived. I loved my parents' room. The window was always open, and the smell of dry fruit was wonderful. Between the two large rooms was a very small room; today one would call it a walk-in closet. Clothes hung overhead, and when I first arrived, I slept on one side under the clothes, and Peter slept on the other side.

Because there was so little room, I remained at Les Vignes for only a few days before moving to Subtray, a very small, poor village nearby. In fact, it wasn't even a real village, just a very simple housing development. Most of the people living there were employed by farmers. The housing units were row houses, and each consisted of one room with a cast-iron stove for cooking and heating, two beds, a table, and a cupboard. I shared a room with a woman who slaughtered animals. She had a very big, sharp knife, and she would come home after a day's work and tell me what she had killed. Sometimes I was afraid of falling asleep because she would arrive home drunk, and I was afraid that she would have a dream and mistake me for an animal she was slaughtering.

Félix was a wonderful friend to my father. They played chess together and sang continuously and monotonously. "I am a cockatoo and you are a kangaroo." They shared the same temperament. The two men sometimes behaved like cheerful boys. So, the atmosphere was never sad. They always tried to keep us happy. It was strange; in the middle of the war, in a little house, they made up funny songs and funny stories and talked funny nonsense. But they were always plotting the next move.

My mother was trying hard to find a way of joining us. For some reason, none of the correspondence we had sent about Peter ever reached her. Later my mother told me that she thought he was dead and was in a deep state of grief. When she walked in the street of Chaville, she sometimes mistook a young man walking in front of her for her son, and the disappointment once she realized it was not Peter was agonizing again and again.

*Left to right:
Marguerite, Jules,
Eve, Félix, Batia*

*Chanukah,
left to right:
Eve, Félix,
Marguerite,
Tili, Batia,
Jules*

*Goldschmidt
children
left to right:
Jules, Eve,
Chmouel
(René), Batia,
Tili*

*False identification paper
issued to Félix Goldschmidt
under the name
Henry Lelievre*

Courtesy of the United States
Holocaust Memorial Museum

*Below: False
identification paper
issued to
Félix Goldschmidt
under the name
Fernand Gauthier*

Courtesy of the
United States Holocaust
Memorial Museum

Chapter Eight
Fleeing to the Free Zone, June 1940

The division between the North and South of France had become a massive abyss for the Kroch family. The demarcation line had just been created in June of 1940 after the defeat of France a month earlier. In order to cross the "green" line from the Occupied Zone of the North to the Free Zone of the South, one needed to obtain a special permit. Very few were granted, and particularly not to Jews.

As the dangers escalated for Jews in Paris, Lore, Grofa, Judith, and Alexandra faced increasing pressure to leave. They watched as their neighbors packed a few belongings and disappeared overnight. Some found places to hide, but most fled to join the swarm migrating south. With no husband to consult, Lore made the decision to join the exodus. She mustered the strength to undertake the dangerous journey to Mézières-en-Brenne in the Free Zone, where she hoped to reunite with the rest of the family. Had she known of the dangers that would befall them, would my grandmother have taken the risk?

Judith

When the German troops marched into Holland without meeting any resistance, we knew that it was only a matter of time before they reached the French border. We were deeply concerned. Our neighbors had already taken off in their packed car a few days after the beginning of the war for points in the south. More and more inhabitants of our town left their homes and moved south. Grofa, Mutti, Alexandra, and I were four women on our own. Fear became contagious.

Finally, when all the neighbors were fleeing on foot, and when there were rumors that the Germans were at the gates of Paris, we went to the Champerais (also known as Gypsies or Roma) and asked for a wheelbarrow. At least five generations of the Champerais lived a few houses away in an ancient building. Not one of them had ever seen a comb. They were the dirtiest people I have ever seen in my life, and also the kindest. They still drew water from a well, an oddity in the suburbs so near to Paris. Their yard around the house, overgrown like a magic garden, was teeming with snakes and scorpions, which were never disturbed except when a bare-footed child stepped on one. The little children wore no diapers, so one had to watch where one stepped. But everyone was happy and helpful. They gave us their wheelbarrow without reservation and wished us good luck, for they knew that as German Jews we were in greater peril than the French.

We packed two suitcases, one for Grofa, and the other was for Mutti, Alexandra, and me. On top we put a couple of blankets and coats as well as the little food we had left. We locked the house and started out in fear and haste, laboriously pushing the cart. Our Grofa was heavy and short of breath. Since childhood she had suffered from a heart defect, which made walking hard for her. After a slow hundred meters, we realized that we would never get anywhere this way. So Grofa, in spite of her protests, was hoisted on top of the cart, and was alternately pushed by Mutti and me.

Alexandra

Before he was interned, Papa Fritz had given each of us a little pocket made of some precursor to plastic; something that was impervious to water. We wore it around our necks, under our clothes, directly on our bodies. In it was a sum of money and a list of addresses. The first one was in Central France, and that was Papa's friend Goldschmidt, who was a French Jew. We wore these packets even at night when we slept. We hid them under our pajamas. It gave me a feeling of security. My father was always an optimist – a "realistic optimist." What I mean by "realistic optimist" is that he foresaw possible difficulties and did his best to ameliorate them. The "realism" was his awareness that we might get separated. But we would always find each other again; that was the optimist part.

Grofa and Mutti and Judith and I started walking with a tide of people: older men, children, and women of all ages. The men of army age weren't represented because they had been drafted to serve in the French army. We had no specific aim. Everybody wanted to get

67

across the Loire River, which cuts France in half. We worried that the bridges across the Loire would be dynamited after the French army was through in order to prevent the Germans from getting across. But we wanted to be on the other side of the Loire when that happened.

People carried what they could. We didn't take much, mostly clothing. But it was still too much. Later we had to get rid of a lot of our clothing and canned food. In some of the villages we passed through, the bakers had stayed behind and baked bread, and given or sold it to the refugees. Grofa wasn't supposed to talk because her French was so bad. She was supposed to be a deaf mute. We didn't want to speak German amongst this mass of humanity fleeing the Germans. When we distanced ourselves and went to a field for something to eat, then we spoke amongst ourselves in German, but we stayed silent in front of the group.

Judith

We had to keep going in the direction of Vélizy-Villacoublay in order to avoid the German army, which was advancing from the north without meeting any resistance. The road to Villacoublay was uphill. We were in trouble not only because of the weight of our beloved Grofa, but also because we were not used to such efforts. More than once the cart threatened to tip over. Having reached the hill opposite Chaville, we stopped for a well-deserved rest. We had hardly covered more than two kilometers but were already battle weary, as if we had spent the entire day on a forced march.

Alexandra

We passed a military airport, and a French soldier saw the four of us with the cart and called us over. I was always the spokesperson for the family because I had the best accent-free, fluent French.

He asked, "Do you want this cart?" He was pulling a "remarque," a wagon that attaches to a car. It was big with two tires and a rest in the back, so you could pull it or you could stand it on its rest, and it would be horizontal. He gave it to us, and we put our possessions on it, and left the little wagon for someone else. When we thanked him, he said he would rather give it to French people than to leave it to the Germans. If only he knew that I was German!

I didn't consider myself German – I was Jewish and stateless. Hitler had revoked all Jews' German citizenship. So, I wasn't even legally German. Even today, when people say, "Oh, you're German," it rubs me the wrong way. I am not German. I was born in Germany, but I am not German. But people are not sensitive to it anymore. And that is a double-edged sword. On the one hand, it is wonderful that people get over these horrors and come together. On the other hand, an elderly person who has experienced those horrors – for me it's not history, it's my life. And the younger generations should be sensitive to that.

When Grofa got tired, she climbed on, and when I got tired, we switched places. Mutti and Judith pulled us. I pushed when I could. The evening of the first night fleeing, we were in a big field near a haystack. There were people smoking, so my mother asked them to stop smoking because it was too dangerous. But they said "no," they'd done it all their lives. So, we moved to another haystack where nobody smoked. We tried to go to sleep there. But it started raining, and the rain smelled like gasoline. It was indeed gasoline because the French had exploded several of their gasoline storage tanks at the airports. The rain brought the condensed fuel down.

So, my mother declared, "I'm not staying near a haystack." We went into a barn, which was already full of people. We slept on straw mats like sardines in a can.

The second night, we ate some canned peas for dinner, and I got very sick. Nobody else got sick, just me. I probably had a fever. I was lying on the little cart, and the others were walking. A man and a boy came over and asked my mother what was wrong with me.

My mother said, "I don't know, but she's sick."

So the little boy handed me half a bar of chocolate, and said, "Because she's sick, I want to share with her," and he walked on. That was the only time I ever saw those people in my life. The thought of chocolate made me sick, but I clutched it because I knew there would be the day when I wanted it. During that night I had nightmares. We were on the main highway, and I was lying on the cart looking up. On either side were large trees with very ominous shapes that looked like threatening animals. They were all very menacing.

Judith

The next morning, Mutti and I pulled this comfortably rolling cart with renewed energy, and soon reached the throng of refugees heading south. The stream of refugees was silent. Whoever becomes part of such a current is carried along by the incessant, moving, amorphous mass. The sense of sharing a common fate, being part of a whole, helped me to pull the cart forward, forward like a dumb ox.

We were hungry and had not slept enough. The farms we passed had been abandoned by their owners, and the animals milled around unattended. The chickens could take care of themselves. They found food. But the cows with their swollen udders mooed pitifully. They were actually screaming, for they had not been milked for days. Some refugees, themselves farmers, helped the poor beasts and distributed the warm milk. Later we came to a village where the bakery had just opened. No sooner was the bread baked than the hungry crowd bought it all. In this way we replenished our meager provisions.

My mother had long since handed the reins over to me, the fourteen-year-old. In her youth she, like all the other girls in her protected circumstances, had always followed the advice of her parents. She greatly valued the judgment of her father. Just out of school, where she had also been told what to do, she married Fritz Kroch, our father. He was seven years her senior, and he shaped her character. They were a harmonious couple. Mutti was not uncritical by any means, but she adjusted herself to her husband, as she had earlier to her father. She never had to make a decision or take independent action. I am a resolute person. It was obvious to me that I had to take charge. On we went, on and on.

It could have been such a wonderful summer's day. The weather was gloriously sunny and bright. We passed through the Vallee de Chevreuse, one of the loveliest valleys around Paris. There was a smell of freshly mown grass. At some point it became too much. When the second day turned into night, and the red sky was illuminated by the burning oil tanks of Villacoublay, I fell onto a heap of gravel by the roadside and was instantly asleep.

The next day we walked on with the never-ending stream of people, and slowly moving vehicles packed with entire families. We were also accompanied by horse carts, and sometimes a lumbering tethered cow or goat temporarily attached itself to us and nibbled at our clothes. We drew some milk from the udder of a goat that had submitted happily. And we found a newborn kitten. We wrapped it in a rain bonnet because the baby cat had a tendency to "rain" from below. For the next two years, Minouche followed us wherever we went, faithful as a little dog.

We were hungry. Alexandra was feeling better, and the two of us went off to find something to eat while Mutti and Grofa stayed with the cart. Suddenly, literally out of the blue, there appeared a low flying plane, which dropped a bomb. It exploded not far from the two of us with such a bang that we were thrown to the ground. We were so shocked that we forgot to get up until Mutti, ashen faced with worry and fright, came running to make sure that we were in one piece. Whether the bomb came accidentally from a German or French plane we will never know.

We reached a huge, fertile plateau, La Beauce, France's granary. Wheat fields stretched from horizon to horizon. In normal times it would have been an imposing sight. Under the circumstances we hardly looked at it. Our sore feet burned like fire in our shoes. The country road, lined by two rows of poplars, led in a straight line to the city of Chartres, and we could already see the famous cathedral. At the sound of approaching planes, people quickly threw themselves into the ditches on the right and the left. Grofa climbed laboriously from the cart and reached the safety of the ditch just before several low flying planes began to direct their machine gun fire at the refugees. This time it was no accident. This was a planned attack on the lives of civilians. The pilots returned to shoot again, but they hit only the pavement, so nobody in our vicinity was hurt. All four of us had crawled into a large culvert linking the ditches on the left and the right. We heard the bullets crackle again and again. Then the ground trembled under the hooves of shying horses breaking away from their fully laden carts. First you could hear them in the distance, then closer and closer. They raced above our heads, sounding like wild drumbeats.

I was lying in the culvert, pulling snails from the walls, as unconcerned as if all this had nothing to do with me. It was an almost euphoric feeling. The planes dropped a few bombs over Chartres, which caused fires to erupt in parts of the town in front of the cathedral. From our road it looked as if the holy church was surrounded by flames. Yet, "Oh miracle," the cathedral itself remained intact amidst the conflagration, as if invulnerable. The devout Christians among us saw this as a sign from the Holy Virgin. They crossed themselves and thanked her. With renewed vigor, we continued on our way.

We passed the medieval, picturesque, scarcely damaged town hoping to be given a chance to see it again in our lifetime. Beyond Chartres, the refugees separated into groups going off in different directions. We kept to the southernmost route. We had long gone beyond the limits of our map. So as not to starve, we had succeeded a few times in trading some clothes, a watch or a piece of jewelry for food.

We walked through the night in silence. Meanwhile, the news had spread by word of mouth that Paris had been occupied by the Germans on June 14. Though this came as no surprise, we felt despondent. All through the warm, moonlit night we heard a constant droning of airplanes.

Grofa was dozing on the cart, which by then had lost much of its load because, to reduce the weight, we had given away or thrown into the ditch everything except Grofa's luggage. Suddenly I saw something. Was it a hallucination? Was I dreaming with my eyes wide open? Was Mutti seeing the same thing? Yes, she was staring in the same direction, along with many of the refugees, at the white balloons gently drifting from the sky. They were not balloons, as we realized when they got closer, but athletic young women and men with parachutes who came gliding noiselessly into the fields around us. They folded their white canopies, set up their collapsible bicycles, and joined our group, all without a sound. We all looked at each other, but nobody said a word. It was a surreal moment. Shivers went up and down my spine. To this day we have no idea what that was about.

We continued for a few more kilometers, and then, disheartened, we collapsed on the ground. The stream of people passed us by. As morning dawned, the weather had changed. It began to rain. We were alone. In the distance we heard cannon fire. Or was it thunder, or both? On the entire plain there was no one except us. Where were the others? What directions would we take?

As the rain came pelting down on us, our "angel" appeared. He was North African, and his eyes looked frightened. His French was poor, and he did not understand what language we were speaking. The little food we had, we shared with him. He took hold of the cart and pulled it with considerable strength until we rejoined the lost herd. We followed him, soaked to the skin. With each step, the water squished in our shoes. Then the angel disappeared without a word. It seemed to us that he had been sent from heaven. We will be grateful to him forever. For me this was proof that angels do exist.

My mother could not go on. She had come to the end of her physical as well as her mental strength. Without her, I was not able to pull the cart. I felt my grandmother's weight doubling with every kilometer.

Alexandra

Suddenly, my mother fainted. There we were by the roadside, all alone. We decided we needed to get help right away. So, we left her with Grofa while Judith and I walked to the nearest abandoned farm, where we found a group of French soldiers together with a group of refugees like ourselves. Judith asked to speak to the boss of this group.

One of the soldiers came forward and said, "I am Marceau Boucheny, and I am a corporal. I am the leader of this group of soldiers, and we have decided to take care of some refugees, because we couldn't help our country militarily. We feel that at least we can take care of some civilians and do some good."

My sister said, "Well, we need you."

Mr. Boucheny replied, "Well, we can't take any more, because we can't secure more people than we already have here."

Judith told them that our mother had fainted, and that we really needed help. So, they came and looked, and decided "yes," they would adopt us, too. That is how we ended up with these soldiers. They picked us up, and they took our cart. At the farm, they milked the cows and gave us milk. We all ate, and it felt much better to be with these people. My mother recovered.

We were with them for two nights. There must have been about five soldiers and twelve refugees. One of them was a monk. There were no other children. We walked every day. During the day, they would go to abandoned farms and find food for us. And at night, they would break into abandoned houses and find beds for us.

They were very kind, very reassuring and very helpful. My mother had decided right from the start that she was going to tell Marceau who we were; that we weren't just ordinary refugees; that we had a little more to worry about since we were Jewish. Later on, the monk knew about us, too. He was a very young monk, with a little hair cut off the top of his head. He came from a cloister where they don't speak. He was so happy to talk, and he found Judith so attractive. Judith was very beautiful.

Judith

The monk was greatly impressed by our strict religious observance. He belonged to the order of Trappists. When they sent him to the army, he was given dispensation permitting him to speak while outside his monastery. They did not imagine that the first person that he would say more than "merci" to would be a Jewish girl.

His name was Jean le Gellec. He was very attracted to me, and I to him. I felt honored and pleased and didn't leave his sight. He was a very good-looking guy. Jean wanted to know all about Jewish customs since he came from a small village in Brittany and had never before met a Jew. We took walks alone together, and he asked me about Jewish holidays and which foods we were permitted and not permitted to eat. He was very impressed that, though we were very hungry, we did not touch food that wasn't kosher. When we saw fried non-kosher chicken on the table, we didn't eat it. We ate the bread. It showed him that we had steadfastness. We knew it would soon end. It was finished the day we said goodbye, forty-eight hours after we met. We never kissed. "No, no, no!" He had already transgressed his laws by talking to me.

Alexandra

In one of the farms we found a car and gasoline. A little way down the road was an abandoned big truck that was absolutely laden with chocolate and slippers. So, we all had wonderful, cozy slippers on our hurting feet and an extra pair or two stashed away, and we had as much chocolate as we could possibly want. Now that we had two vehicles, everybody was seated in the car or the truck, and we drove off. We were still north of the Loire, and we stopped in the woods to rest.

At that very moment, German soldiers rolled in on their tanks and trucks in large numbers, yelling, "The war's over, we've won the war, go home, go home, go home." We were stunned.

As we were trying to organize what to do next, a German soldier came over and commanded the French soldiers who were with us, "This is what you do." He took the rifles from our French soldiers and broke them on the ground so that they were in two pieces.

"And then you go to the prisoner of war camp, and you turn yourselves in as prisoners."

Judith

Fortunately, we had taken the precaution earlier to gather Grofa's German passport and our identity papers and burn them. The passport had been stamped with a big "J" (for Jew), and the name "Sarah" had been added to all our papers by the German authorities in 1938, so that everyone could see at a glance that they were dealing with a Jew. For men the additional name was "Israel."

Very politely, in their best high school French, the Germans told Marceau and his men to go immediately to an assembly camp in a nearby town. Our friends did not have the slightest intention of becoming prisoners of war. Instead, they opened a few homes, removed their uniforms, took some shirts and suits out of the wardrobes, asked the owners' forgiveness under their breath, and returned to us in fresh civilian clothes. Somewhere along the road, someone found a car without gas; someone else found gas without a car. Everything was for the taking.

As we were driving on towards the south, we suddenly came upon long lines of refugees on their way back north. They told us that all the bridges across the River Loire had been blown up by the retreating French. Without a moment's hesitation, Marceau invited us all to his father's place, in Aulnay-la-Rivière, a tiny village of one hundred fifty people twenty kilometers away. He entered the house, named "Le Paradis," first to greet his family.

Alexandra

Marceau came out with his father and threw open the gate – a great big iron gate.

His father, Pépé, stood there with his arms spread wide and said, "Welcome, everybody. Come in." Meanwhile, his mother, Mémé, had already started to cook for all fifteen people.

The first night, we all slept in the Moulin de la Groue, a little way down the road from the farm, an old abandoned water mill, near the little stream where I learned to swim. We slept on the straw scattered on the floor. The next morning, after breakfast, all the others left to return to their homes. We stayed with Marceau's parents, and he returned to his tiny house in the next village, four kilometers down the road, where he lived with his wife, Madeleine, and daughter, Monique, who was a couple of years older than me.

Pépé and Mémé's farm had a stable with one horse, called Gamin, a bay horse, who pulled the wagon when Pépé went into the fields. Gamin shared the stable with a spotted goat, and she was my favorite. When I came into her stall, she always welcomed me with "ma-a-a-ah." I always felt that this was her special greeting for me, and I loved her.

The Essonne, a small stream nearby, is where Marceau taught me how to swim. He knotted a towel across my chest and across my back, and then he took a big pole – probably eight or ten feet long – and knotted a rope at the end of it, and then that rope was tied to the towel around my chest, at the back. First, he had shown me what I had to do with my arms and legs on dry land. Then I walked into the stream, and he walked along the shore with his pole, and I was dangling in the

76

water. He told me at several points that he was going to let the rope go slack, "but if you start to sink, I'll pull you out, so don't be afraid." And after a while he said, "I have not helped you – you have learned by yourself."

Judith

Where else could we have gone? The address hanging neatly wrapped around our necks was that of our friend Félix and his family in Mézières-en-Brenne. We could no longer get there because of the blown-up bridges. The other members of our group left for their destinations the next day.

It was not just named Le Paradis. For us it really was paradise. Pépé and his wife, Mémé, took us in as if we were their most beloved relatives. Pépé had been a customs officer in Algiers. He was a tolerant man and quite cultured. After retiring, he came to live on his small family farm. He had a lively little horse and a few chickens. He cultivated just enough land to feed Gamin, his horse. Like all good farming Frenchmen, he had a little vineyard, which produced a somewhat acid wine, and a number of fruit trees. The main source of food, however, was a narrow stream at the end of the garden where, in the evening, a trap would be set. The next morning it would be full of little fish. Vegetables and fish are kosher, and this is what we ate. After every meal, Mémé put the plates on the floor, where the dogs and cats licked them clean. The pets were part of the family, after all.

Marceau, his only child, was a violinist employed by the well-known Orchestre Pasdeloup in Paris. As a hobby he studied the German language and was therefore pleased to be able to use it. Madeleine, his wife, was a very quiet, refined woman from Lorraine. Our friendship with their daughter, Monique, remained strong throughout her lifetime.

We played in the garden in front of the house, where we collected large vineyard snails, which our hosts ate as a special delicacy. Everything could have been lovely had it not been for the Germans. After about a week of untroubled days, some Germans were quartered in Pépé's barn. To our horror, we discovered that these young men all came from Saxony, our region of Germany, and we were afraid that among them there might be one who knew us. Yet we were not allowed

77

to show our fear. Life was to go on normally.

We lived without papers. Officially we were relatives of the family and therefore did not speak German. This, of course, created some amusing situations. As we walked down the road one day, a soldier asked my mother in German if she had some Salat (salad) to sell. Mutti looked at him as if she had never heard that word. In fact, the French word is salade. He kept on repeating "salat, salat." We just shook our heads and looked at him with vacant eyes until he left us alone. Even when silent, we had to be careful.

One day, Alex, Monique, and I were playing hopscotch, and the German soldiers were sitting on the wall watching us, when one of them remarked, "Those are Jewish children," in typical strong Saxon dialect. My heart missed a beat, but we continued to play as if we had not heard a thing because we didn't want the soldiers to discover that we understood them. A little later we went into the house and told Mutti what had happened, and we never played in the presence of the soldiers again.

Since the only water pump was located in the kitchen, the soldiers came in any time they needed water. From time to time, they exchanged a few words with Marceau. On one occasion there was a knock at the door, and two polite soldiers appeared and asked Marceau for a chair. The word in German is stuhl; however their Saxonian dialect was beyond Marceau's understanding. We were not allowed to help.

When the first soldier realized he was not understood, the second one swaggered forward saying, "You wait, let me take care of this," In an affected voice, but still in broad Saxon he shouted, "'Do you perhaps have some seating accommodation?" Marceau remained confused. He had never come across the term "'seating accommodation" in his German studies. We were not allowed to laugh.

After the soldiers moved on, we found many letters that they had left behind in the barn. I read one from a mother of a German soldier in which she proudly announced to her son that his brother had "been permitted" to die for the Führer and fatherland. Not "He died," or "He had to die." According to her, it was a privilege to be allowed to die for the Fuhrer. Did she really mean to write that, or was she forced to?

The Germans had begun to organize everything and required that all members of every household be registered. Pépé and Mémé had done enough for us. We could not further endanger them. Marceau and Madeleine cycled about a hundred kilometers to Paris and visited our little house in Chaville. They got in touch with our friends and the police of Chaville, who suggested that we should return to Chaville, because otherwise we would not receive food rationing cards.

That was easier said than done. There was no regular train service, and Grofa would not ride a bicycle. Two or three times we set out for the train station in the horse-drawn cart, only to return to Le Paradis because the expected train was not coming. When it finally did arrive, it was so full that we had to fight for a little space in a corner. I stood at the window and held my breath as the train balanced on temporary, newly laid rails across an improvised bridge, held up by wooden supports high above a river.

Paris looked very different. The city was unscathed but full of Wehrmacht (armed forces of Nazi Germany). And there were street signs in German. Sadly, we returned to Chaville. First, we registered with the police of Chaville. They were very friendly and issued us new papers. Summer was coming to an end. The nights became cold, and we were hungry. My father often quoted a piece of Yiddish wisdom that goes like this: "To have no money is no problem. To have no money at all, that is a terrible problem." We had no money at all. "Madam Kroch," my mother, still wearing her elegant clothes from Germany, went to a different fishmonger at a different market every day and asked for carp heads for our cats. Then we ate the fish heads ourselves. She picked up cabbage leaves and other edibles that the French, who were still spoilt at that time, refused to eat. We were too hungry to be fastidious.

When winter came, it turned unusually cold. We had little fuel left, and in order to economize, we left only a very small flame burning in the stove overnight. Little did we know that the flue was not drawing properly, and we almost died of carbon monoxide poisoning. We slept two to a bed (and not a wide one at that) because it was warmer that way, and because we did not have enough beds.

As time passed, it became clear that my father had been right when he gave us all Félix Goldschmidt's address in Mézières-en-Brenne. In 1940, only the northern half of France was occupied by the German troops. Mézières-en-Brenne was situated in the so-called "Free

Zone," in the southern half of France. The Red Cross had introduced preprinted postcards where one could complete the text and add a few words. Something like this: "I/we are well/not well. We are living in ..." For the Germans, this type of card simplified the task of censoring correspondence between the two zones. In this way we learned that Papa, released from camp, had already arrived at Félix's. Eva, too, still almost a child, had resolutely battled her way to Mézières-en-Brenne, thanks to the address hanging around her neck. But we had not heard from Peter.

Our situation was unbearable. We had to find a way of leaving for the Free Zone. Once again there was a dilemma. In order to obtain a pass, without which we couldn't travel, we had to venture into the lion's den, meaning the German High Command in Paris. What Jew would have wanted to do that? There were also passeurs, who smuggled people across the border. However, that cost a lot of money. We didn't have any. We had no choice but to make our way to the German High Command at the Hotel Lutecia. (Lutecia was the original name of the city of Paris). When my mother and I arrived, we saw such a crowd waiting there that we went back home and decided to return to Paris the next morning by the first train from Chaville. The German occupation forces had declared a curfew from 6 p.m. to 6 a.m., so that we were unable to be at the hotel before 8:40. Of course, there were already several hundred French people waiting in a long queue. The office in question was open until noon. We had no place where we could spend the night in Paris. How could we ever get the pass we so wanted?

On the right side in front of the High Commander stood the French citizens; on the left there was a special entrance for diplomats and German nationals. Our German passports had been reduced to ashes. We were neither French citizens nor diplomats. Therefore, we were foreigners. Boldly and with pounding hearts, we joined the line on the left, which led to the special entrance.

Alexandra

When they got to the door, they were stopped by a young soldier. My mother was at the time in her early forties and looked younger and was very beautiful. And Judith was also very beautiful.

"Are you Jewish?" the soldier asked my mother.

"Yes," she responded.

"Then you don't have to go upstairs, because Jews haven't been getting exit permits for the last three weeks."

My mother smiled at him and said, "Do you mind very much if I get thrown out by an officer?"

The soldier smiled back. "No, go right on up."

So, my mother went up, and was ushered into an office, with an officer behind a big desk. There was also a female soldier, who was what the French people called a "gray mouse," souris grise, because they wore gray uniforms. She was a secretary. There were armchairs in front of the desk for the visitors, but they weren't invited to sit.

The officer asked, "What is your name?"

My mother told him, "Kroch." He immediately sent out the souris grise when he heard the name.

"Bitte, Frau Kroch, would you please sit down, and if this is your daughter, would you please sit down." Then he asked which brother Kroch my mother was the wife of, Hans, Curt, or Fritz. This man, Lieutenant Blunk, had been a customer of my father's – an egg farmer from the Leipzig area. He had stored eggs for years in my father's refrigeration houses and had made a good living off my father, and my father had profited from him. Lieutenant Blunk never doubted for a moment that Fritz Kroch was an honest man and a good Jew. And before him was Mr. Kroch's wife, and he felt that he could do something.

Then he made out the papers. He apologized first because my mother couldn't take any of her belongings with her. My mother stretched out her hands to show him her wedding ring and ruby ring and said, "That's all I have." She was about to take it off.

"Aber nein, (but no!), Frau Kroch. You may keep it."

She replied, "The rest you already kept; I don't have anything else."

"Ja, ja, I understand." Then he apologized a second time, and he put a great big red "J" on the papers for Grofa, Judith, Mutti, and me to leave. He apologized, but explained that he had to add the "J."

Judith

Very surprised, relieved and elated, we returned to Chaville. Once again Marceau and Madeleine came to our assistance. They brought us something to eat and money for the tickets, and stayed with us for the two days as we waited for the train to take us south. On the train, we had an entire compartment to ourselves and could stretch out, a great comfort after all those painful hours waiting on the platform of the Gare de Lyon in Paris.

Towards morning, the train stopped at Châteaudun, on the demarcation line dividing the occupied area from the Free Zone. Many a Jewish traveler was taken off the train here and not heard of again. We had to give our travel documents, duly signed by Lieutenant Blunk, to the conductor. Now we were waiting nervously for the border guards to come and search our luggage or to interrogate us. We heard voices, fast steps, travelers getting on and off.

Alexandra

A border guard approached us. He did not believe that these were legitimate papers. So, my mother said to him, "Why would I put a 'J' on if I had faked it? I will pay you to make a phone call ... my money. You call Lieutenant Blunk, who signed this paper, and ask him whether they're real. You make the call."

So he made the call, and when he came back, the officer said, "You can go."

Judith

Mézières-en-Brenne is a small town in the department of Indre. Its capital is Châteauroux, and that is as far as the train from Paris would take you. There we changed to a local train that brought us to Buzançais, where we boarded a yet smaller train, which trudged along so slowly that we could have gotten off to pick flowers while it was in motion. At last we were in Mézières-en-Brenne. The family was united.

Abandoned car and the Kroch's trailer

Communication with censored postcards

Le Paradis, Aulnay-la-Rivière

*Pépé with refugees. Sitting at left, Pépé with mustache; second row right
kneeling, Marceau; third row from right to left, standing, Lore Kroch, two
unknown ladies; standing, tall, young monk, Judith, Monique, Grofa,
Madeleine; in front of Grofa and Madeleine part of Alexandra's face, two
unknown ladies; standing behind, Mémé*

Chapter Nine
Mézières-en-Brenne, 1940-1942

Mézières-en-Brenne had (and continues to have) a population of about one thousand inhabitants, of which three hundred lived in the village, and the remainder on nearby farms. The Catholic church was in the center of the village. There was a well in the town square where the weekly market was held, next to the pharmacy and the police station. It was a non-descript village in the middle of nowhere ... which is exactly why Félix Goldschmidt chose it as his home to hide out during the war.

The plastic pouch containing Goldschmidt's address had guided the Kroch family to this safe haven. Each member of the family had endured a harrowing journey to this prearranged place of refuge. And they were now, miraculously reunited.

Judith

Grete and Félix Goldschmidts' house, "Les Vignes" (The Vineyard), was three kilometers from Mézières-en Brenne. In addition to the kitchen on the ground floor there were two rooms upstairs. The Goldschmidts and their five children slept in the larger room. They had given their bedroom to my parents. Peter camped on the landing. There was so little space that in the evenings the three sisters and Grofa slept in a room in the neighboring village of Subtray consisting of five houses. There were no toilets, only outhouses. We used newspaper for toilet paper. Grofa had trouble getting us girls out of bed in the morning, for when the temperature is ten degrees Celsius it is a dreadful thought to have to leave a warm bed and have to wash in a basin of ice-cold water in an unheated room. To get us up she would recite,

"Arise my child, and seek delight
While summertime is reigning bright ..."

For over a year we lived peaceably together. The first winter food was scarce. Peter went out on his bicycle to scour the surrounding countryside for something to eat. The daily bread ration for seven people was half a kilo (just over a pound). My father cut the round loaf of whole grain meal and sawdust as best he could into seven equal pieces, which were distributed by drawing lots. We could do what we liked with our own rations, which were the size of a wedge of pie. Some would eat it all at once. Others spread it out and ate it bit by bit throughout the day. Some kept it till evening. No, not really. No one could wait that long. We spread the boiled down juice of rotten beets (the fresh ones were fed to the horses) and congratulated ourselves for having found this marvelous substitute for jam. To me it tasted like shoe polish, but I wasn't allowed to say that.

One holiday we obtained oat flakes from the grocery store. Real oat flakes, unbelievable! Delighted, we sat down at the table, and all the children began to eat with gusto. Suddenly my sharp eyes discovered that every third oat flake was in fact a maggot. That was the reason why our grocer had sold them to us so kindly, at full price. Just as I was about to let out a scream of disgust, Marguerite Goldschmidt, who was standing behind me, put her hand over my mouth. She took me aside and explained that the children were undernourished and would be better off eating boiled maggots than going hungry. I could not touch my porridge, in spite of nagging hunger.

During the winter, it was most terrible because we had no garden, and nothing was growing. Spoiled cattle turnips were boiled, roasted or mashed. Most of the time, we went to sleep hungry, and we often cried on the way to our bedroom. This was one of the worst parts I remember about the war. People who have felt hunger know that it is a pain in your stomach that doesn't leave you for a minute, and you have no saliva. You feel like a completely different person and can't think of anything except eating.

On my father's forty-eighth birthday, January 26, 1941, my brother was able to bring home one egg, for which he had spent two days working. We presented it to Papa with great ceremony. It was hard boiled and distributed among the children – one bite each.

There were other good moments, too. We loved Mézières-en-Brenne and its friendly inhabitants. Our house stood alone, far back from the road. To the right and the left there were large fields, and behind us were woods. All around us was nothing but untouched nature. The winter was hunting season. To the sound of reverberating bugle calls and the yelping of dogs, the ladies and gentlemen rode into the forest to hunt fox, pheasant, and hare, and occasionally even a wild boar. Eventually our indefatigable brother began to bring more food home from the farms. As soon as the snow melted, Grofa went into the fields behind the house and with a sharp knife cut the first green shoots of stinging nettles and cooked us a delicious dish.

Eva

When my mother, sisters, and Grofa arrived, all of us except our mother moved into to a larger room in the Subtray housing settlement. She stayed with the Goldschmidts along with Peter and our Papa. We had three beds to share among the four of us. Alexandra slept with me, and Grofa and Judith each had a bed. There was a big kitchen stove, some chairs, a cupboard, and a table, a chamber pot, and a sack of potatoes.

One winter morning we woke up and the room was completely dark. We knew it was morning, but in the room, it was night. We were snowed in. The snow was above the level of the door and the window. Both the door and the wooden window shutters opened to the outside, so there was no way to get out. We cooked a few potatoes and stayed in our beds for warmth. It was like being in a house of ice. I remember the cold. I always had cold fingers and toes and was afraid they would freeze. Towards midday, Peter and Papa arrived from the big house in Mézières. They had to dig a path through a kilometer of snow to get to us and shovel us out.

Though the three sisters and our grandmother slept at Subtray, Les Vignes is where we always had our meals together with the Goldschmidt family. We often ate topinambour, which is Jerusalem artichoke – a small, lumpy root vegetable with a thin skin. When it's cooked, it becomes soft, glassy and sweet. We added onions and leeks to our meal for Shabbat, and that was a big treat.

After our first winter, we bought very small chickens that were sold in cartons. Each chicken was nestled in a small mold, the way we buy eggs today; and we nurtured them through their various stages of growing up. We had Colette Brune and Colette Blanche. Colette Brune had a collar of brown feathers, and Colette Blanche a collar of white. Colette Brune was the cleverest hen we ever had, a natural leader. She always found worms and grains, and the others ran after her. She was always the first to arrive when we fed them. There were a few cocks but only one really impressive one, Casimir, who grew and grew and became more and more beautiful. He had marvelous colors and a huge tail, and the hens adored him. The other cocks didn't have a chance, poor things. We had hens for eggs, and for meat on weekends. This was our only source of meat. But Casimir was also eaten in the end.

Then there was Pied Pied, who sat in his paper mold a little sad because his foot had been broken somehow, and so he started life with a crooked foot and a limp. He was doubly unfortunate because he drowned in the rainwater tub, and when he drowned, it was a day of mourning for us.

Behind the house we planted corn to feed the chickens, and in front of the house we planted tomatoes, beans, leeks, and lettuce. In the morning, we drew lots to decide who should sit at the window that overlooked the country road. The others stood by behind the hedge with a bucket and spade. Cows and horse-drawn wagons passed quite frequently, and what the animals dropped we put in our bucket. We didn't want the farmers to see us because we were embarrassed. They had heaps of manure on their farms, and we didn't want to beg them for any. So, when no one was around, we hopped into the road and filled the bucket. We dug holes for our tomatoes and filled them with our manure before putting young tomato plants in the ground that we had grown from seed. The farmers never understood why the Krochs had bigger, redder tomatoes than anyone else. They wondered what our secret was. Did we say a special prayer?

We also dried apples and strung up beans to dry. We passed a thick thread through the beans and made a knot between each bean so that they wouldn't touch each other while they were drying. We hung them in the sun by the hundreds. We learned some of these ways to preserve from the farmers, but mostly from our mother. Her brother Anshelm had been a nature lover and had a wide knowledge of plants and flowers that he passed to his sister, our mother. There was hardly a flower that she couldn't identify by name, and she knew where things grew. This knowledge of the secrets of nature, together with her phenomenal memory (which went in a straight line from her mother to her to me), helped us when we had to rely on our resources to keep ourselves fed.

We looked for milk to buy because we made our own butter. The whole family sat around and shook a large milk container until a lump of butter formed. We drank the buttermilk, and the butter we ate on bread, which wasn't real bread. The husks of the grain that were usually thrown away or used to reinforce animal food were made into "bread," resulting in bread that was very hard and brittle and stuck in our throats.

Blackberry bushes grew close to the country road. The local inhabitants didn't eat the blackberries because they believed they brought lice into the house. They had other superstitions. For instance, if you laid a loaf of bread on its back with the flat side on top, this brought the devil into the house. So, nobody except us ate blackberries, and when they were in season, we picked them by the bucketful, ate them raw, cooked them for dessert, or made good jam. And so, we ate bad bread with good butter, and good jam.

The relationship among all of us was very good. We talked and sang, and when Peter accompanied us on his violin, it was even more enjoyable. Peter was a wonderful brother. He was very peace loving and on good terms with everyone. He never put on airs, never made us feel that he thought himself superior to us. When we needed him, he was always there for his sisters. He did something very touching when we lived together. He would go from one bed to the other and fold our clothes and put them on a chair. His own clothes would be thrown around, but for his sisters, it had to be right. And he loved to sit and tell us stories, stories about "Woolle Wollee," a little boy. They always began with "Wollee Wollee crossed the street ..."

During the summer I sometimes went for an evening walk with my father. He wanted to get out, and nobody wanted to go with him, so I went. We walked and hardly spoke.

Once I asked my mother, "Papa is always so angry with me. And why is Grofa also angry with me? Why does she always say, "It's Eva's fault?"

"With your grandmother it always had to be somebody's fault," my mother responded. "You must try to understand it. Peter is the only son. For your father he is everything, also for your grandmother. And Alexandra; she is the baby of the family. Papa loves his baby, and Grofa would never dare say anything against her. And if one would have said anything bad to Judith, she would open her mouth and give back as good as she got. So that leaves you, Eva. You are the only one patient enough to put up with it. Please go on being patient, for the sake of peace in the family." I accepted what she said, and that is why it remained that way.

On the one side of the country lane was a forest, and on the other were big meadows. Each was bordered by trees on three sides. As my father and I walked along the open sides, it was as if we were going past a number of large, open stages. In the light of the August evenings, these meadows, with trees at the far end on both sides, were all shades of green, ranging from light yellowish to almost deep blue. And it seemed that every branch, every leaf of these richly varied trees and bushes was clearly visible.

Every tree seemed to hold a choir of nightingales. The song of the nightingale is something quite special. It is not a chirping. It begins deep down and goes up, up, up in trills and goes down again, rather like a theme from Wagner's "Flying Dutchman." I was convinced that the song of the nightingale was Wagner's inspiration. It begins in a minor key, rises slowly, and become deeper and fuller in waves, like going forward two or three steps and one step back, almost tragically. The nightingales didn't all sing at once; they began at different intervals. My father and I found ourselves in a grand display of trills and music. Their sound has a sobbing effect that touches the heart. That is why nightingales are so loved.

My father at last found a small house to rent called Les Troènes, where our family could all live together. My parents moved from Les Vignes, where they had been living with the Goldschmidts, and the rest of us joined them from Subtray. The house had never been lived in. The owner, who lived in Paris, had built it as a summer house and hadn't had the money to finish it completely. He had given it to a lawyer to rent out for him. It had neither running water nor electricity; just three small rooms, a kitchen, and a bathroom with a toilet. In one tiny room slept

Peter and my grandmother in bunk beds. We had a living room with a sofa, a table, and a few stools. At night my parents slept on the sofa. In the other small bedroom Alexandra, Judith and I slept in a bunk bed or on a "floor bed." There was a wonderful cherry tree in the garden. In France, the cherries are heaven. Apart from the tree, the garden was bare earth.

The first thing we did when we moved into Les Troènes was to ask the farmer who lived closest to us if we could take water from his well. He agreed with grace. In order to reach the well in his yard, we had to walk half a kilometer there and half a kilometer back. The four children would fill two gray metal bath-shaped tubs that had a handle at each end, as well as two buckets. Then we carried the water back, two to each tub. We had to fetch water twice a day, and that was hard work, but it wasn't at all unbearable.

When we got home, we filled pots with the water for cooking on the iron stove. The water that was not boiled was used for washing dishes and anything else that needed cleaning, including ourselves. It was all very simple and very primitive. In those days, people in France did not bathe so much. There were official bath houses. If you were a clean person, you went there once a week. We went to Mézière to bathe every Friday. We would go into a little bathroom, get a clean towel and a piece of soap, and then remain inside for about a quarter of an hour.

In the evenings, Peter fetched his violin, and we sat in front of the house. The sisters sang in harmony, and Peter played while our parents watched us from their upstairs window, my father with his arm around my mother. Peter played beautiful old French folk songs, as well as melodies from Beethoven, including the chorus from the Ninth Symphony. They had been set to words, and we sang in French. This was a wonderful memory.

We were usually in a good mood, and that was because our parents were always optimistic and in good spirits. My father was full of fun, and my mother loved this and responded to it. Many years later, she told me how happy she had been to see him so optimistic, and how it had affected her.

She said, "It is wonderful for a woman when her husband is reassuring and hopeful."

Judith

It cannot be said that we now lived in luxurious circumstances. Electricity was available in Mézières-en-Brenne, but it had not yet been installed in Les Troènes. Gas stoves or gas heaters were not yet known. We got along very well without a telephone, record player, or radio. By the light of a smelly carbide lamp, we spent our evenings singing. When we ran out of songs, we made up our own.

During the winter, it was dreadfully cold. We warmed ourselves by heating water on the wood stove in the kitchen. It took hours. Then we poured the water into empty bottles. They served as our individual heaters until the water got cold. We had no dry wood to burn in the stove, since we had not collected it the previous summer. Green wood filled the kitchen with acrid smoke, which irritated our eyes.

None of us felt like doing the dishes in the smoky mini kitchen. Who would want to wash dirty plates in a basin with lukewarm water and baking soda? They simply didn't get clean. Once in a while, one needed a toilet or a bath. The former was possible, though without a flushing mechanism. A pail of water did the job. There was no such thing as a bath. The owner of the house obviously never had the intention of taking a bath. We put a small basin, dubbed the Fink Schüssel (finch bowl), in front of the toilet. There was not enough room for a larger basin. So as not to undress in public, we learned to wash from head to toe under our clothes, using six cups of water. We were not very clean, but that was the best we could do.

Alexandra

We had a chamber pot for the night with a great big, blue eye painted inside. Grofa didn't like that very much. We thought it was funny, but she didn't like the eye looking up her gown. For lighting we had carbide, and it smelled awful. It's a chemical solid which, when united with water, creates a terribly smelly gas and makes a fairly bright light. In the light of our carbide lamp, we played cards – the Kroch family game of Gin Rummy.

Eva often told me to straighten up. She kept bugging me that I wasn't sitting up straight or standing straight enough. I must have been fourteen. Eva, Judith, and I had bunk beds in one room. We had no running water. And when we needed to wash ourselves, we washed in a tub right in our bedroom. We poured water over ourselves as we stood in the tub. At that age, I was very conscious of my body. And when I wanted to wash, no one was allowed to come in the room. One day, Eva said she absolutely had to come in immediately.

And I said," All right, don't look at me," and turned my body to the wall.

She looked at me, despite having said she wouldn't, and said, "I have to call Mutti; there's something wrong with your back." And Mutti came in and saw that I had scoliosis.

For a while on Fridays, when we still could get a little flour, Grofa baked challah bread for Shabbat, and that was an all-day operation. One couldn't disturb her. We were not allowed to open the kitchen door from the beginning to the end of the baking, and when Grofa came out of that kitchen in the evening, after a whole day in the overheated kitchen, her face was the color of a tomato, with her yellow hair on top.

On Friday mornings, Judith, the only brave one in the family, walked the five kilometers to Goldschmidt, who was a shochet, which means he had a license to be able to kill animals the Jewish ritual way. So, Judith took the live chicken or rooster to Goldschmidt and came back with a fully plucked, edible-looking piece of meat. That was our meat: one chicken, once a week, for all seven of us.

We were very hungry. Hungry enough to eat rationed bread that was gray and moldy and hard. And hungry enough to make soup out of nettles that we picked. Goldschmidt made molasses out of Jerusalem artichoke. Peter worked on the farms for no money, just for whatever food they were willing to give him at the end of a day of very hard work. Sometimes he brought home potatoes that were not quite good enough to give to the pigs. That first winter was really, really bad.

Minouche was still with us, our very faithful and obedient cat. When we called, she came from wherever she was outdoors; she was mostly an outdoor cat. She fed herself because we didn't have much food to give her.

Eva

One day, in the middle of spring, when the cherries were ripe, Mr. Hollman, the owner of the house, arrived. He was a miserable person, a French Nazi. He wore boots and was full of self-importance.

He knocked loudly and announced, "I am the owner and I want you to leave!" He had not known before that his house had been rented to Jews, and he was furious.

My father replied, "No, I paid in advance, and nobody can make us get out. Go to the mayor, go to the lawyer, nobody can throw us out. We will stay as long as we pay, and also as long as we want to stay." The owner made a lot of noise and called the police.

The police came and said, "This is none of our business. There is nothing we can do!"

Then he shouted, "You are picking my cherries. Don't you dare pick my cherries! This is my tree, and these are my cherries, and you are not allowed to pick them."

My father calmly replied, "Of course you can pick them and take them with you. But as long as we live here and pay, we are entitled to the fruit as much as you are."

The man became more and more insulting, and suddenly my father acted out a comedy. There was no wallpaper on the walls. They were bare except for a line around the walls, some distance from the floor, which indicated the owner had planned to put paneling on the bottom, and wallpaper from the line, upward. The landlord stood in the little room, and behind him were two policemen who knew my father well and were on friendly terms with him. The owner was shouting and threatening.

Suddenly my father went to the wall, drew his finger along the line that demarcated the planned paneling, and chanted "La-la-la-la oops," and at the "oops" his finger slid down where the line ended. Up he came again to find the next line, "La-la-la-la oops" and again his finger slid down. The whole scene was more than odd; the landlord shouting, the policemen smiling, my father singing nonsense as he traced the top of the panel.

Then the man started screaming about the cherry tree again, and my father began to jump up and down rhythmically like a jumping jack, arms up and down at his sides, legs apart and together, bouncing from one leg to the other and sang, "Our dear God made cherries for the whole world, God made cherries. The cherries come from God." My father, whom everyone knew as a wise, knowledgeable man, who usually weighed his words carefully before he spoke, was behaving like a clown, like a child.

In the end, the policemen burst out laughing and said to the landlord, "Don't you see that you are making a fool of yourself? Go home! Mr. Kroch doesn't owe you any money. He paid in advance."

Alexandra

When Hollman left, he went to the mayor and said, "You've rented my house to a madman." And the mayor said, "That man is not crazy, that is an intelligent man!" We were all in awe of my father. We were all watching in total awe as this was happening.

The Morissé farm is where we spent a lot of time, and where Peter worked. The Morissé family was very good to us, and we became friends. They had a daughter, Jeanine, who was at that time nineteen and had a four-year-old daughter named Huguette. One day Jeanine told us that the other girls from the village thought Jews had tails. They had never met a Jew, and they thought Jews were sort of devilish. Jeanine came to tell us, "I don't believe that, but they believe it." Eva, Judith, and I decided on the spot that we were going to show them. So we all went into the bedroom and showed these girls what we looked like, that we didn't have tails. Then they believed it.

Eva

In the Morissés' house behind closed doors, we danced. These were salon dances. Nobody looked very elegant, but people dressed up looking nice and clean after work. The girls wore work skirts, and boys wore long trousers. There were no jeans then. Sometimes groups of entertainers passed through the area. They weren't real actors or gypsies, but poor folk who came and went. They would set up a fair with booths, or would act out a play, or play music. My siblings and I would attend with a group of village youth whom we had gotten to know through our friends the Morissé children.

The Goldschmidt's house in Mézières, Les Vignes. Note outside stairway, where many old and contemporary photographs were taken.

The Goldschmidt family in the staircase of the "Les Vignes" home in Mézières-en-Brenne: Marguerite, Batia, Eve, Jules, Tili, Chmouel (René)

Chapter Ten
Hiding, Late 1942

Eventually the "Statuts des Juifs" (the laws limiting the rights of Jews) applied to foreign born as well as French Jews, whether they lived in the occupied or unoccupied zones. The Nazi regime, intent on carrying out the "final solution" (the extermination of all Jews), demanded that the French round up thirty thousand Jews for deportation to concentration camps. The Vichy government agreed to deport ten thousand from the unoccupied zone and twenty thousand from the occupied zone. This came to a catastrophic crescendo on July 16 and 17, 1942. During this two-day period, in a spirit of zealous cooperation, the French police collected and handed over seven thousand Jewish women, men, and children from Paris and the surrounding towns.

Though the German order was to hand over only adults, the Vichy government offered to deliver children as well.[14] The decision to have the children killed along with their parents was much more practical for the French authorities, primarily because they wouldn't have known what to do with so many orphans.

The families with children under the age of 16 were first imprisoned in a holding facility in Paris, near the Eiffel Tower, called "the Vélodrome d'Hiver," also known as Vél'd'Hiv. In that place of hell, eight thousand Jews, including four thousand children, endured subhuman conditions for almost a week. There had been no arrangements made for food, water, or bathrooms. Some went into shock; some went crazy; others died. When it was time to be deported, the children were wrenched from their parents, including the infants, and then endured a three-day journey in a cattle car to Auschwitz. Those who survived the agonizing journey without their parents were immediately gassed upon arrival.[15]

Deportations of Jews from France continued until August 1944. Eventually seventy-seven thousand Jews living in France were killed in concentration camps, the majority of them at Auschwitz.[16]

The Kroch family were in increasing danger by living openly as Jews. Determining whom to trust became a matter of life or death.

Judith

The Germans had occupied all of France. People had told us that Jews who were arrested were deported to labor camps in Eastern Europe. No one knew anything definite. Every evening we went to the neighbors. There the windows were closed and the curtains drawn, and the radio was turned on to hear the BBC news in French from London. This was strictly forbidden by the occupied forces. We couldn't understand much because the jamming of the radio frequencies by the Germans was so strong. But just to hear the voice of General de Gaulle (the representative of the Free France) speaking to us from London gave us all courage and hope.

There was a map on the wall where pins marked the retreat of the German troops from Russia after many bloody battles. We began to hope that we might yet await the end of the war quietly in Mézières. But it was not to be. The Vichy government under Marshal Petain, who made deals with the Germans, decided it would now allow all the Jews whom he had initially protected to be deported to Germany. In July 1942, the first to be arrested were French Jews without valid papers. Next came the foreign Jews, and finally all were taken, including French Jews with papers. We belonged to the second group.

One day in late September, shortly before the High Holidays-Rosh Hashanah, our New Year, and Yom Kippur, the Day of Atonement, a policeman from Mézières passed in front of our little garden on his bicycle. I was picking tomatoes and did not even look up. Unobtrusively he called me to the fence and said, "You must disappear immediately because we have just received orders to arrest you. Mais moi, je n'ai rien dit," he whispered. ("But I didn't say anything.") With these words he ended his warning. We had dreaded this day.

Henri Morissé, our farmer friend, had promised that in an emergency he would hide us in his vineyard. We packed a few essentials, including woolen blankets, and left immediately. When the policemen arrived at our house sometime later, they would declare in good faith that the Kroch family had disappeared. They did not make much of an effort to find us.

The vineyard where we hid was far away from any habitation. In any case, no one would have looked for us there, for the dimensions of the wooden shed in his vineyard were such that you could not expect a family of seven to hide inside. It was just short of seven feet square and seven feet high – a big, windowless crate intended to be a tool shed. The farmer had built a horizontal division inside at the height of four feet, which provided an attic that could be reached through a hole. He had cleared out the attic for us and provided a pail for sanitary purposes. Nobody could stand. "Upstairs" we could barely sit. Therefore, we slept most of the time. During the day we kept absolutely quiet because there were workers in the vineyard. As soon as it was dark, Mr. Morissé came with a pot full of potatoes boiled in their skins and some hard-boiled eggs. We crawled out of our hut, stretched our limbs and experienced wonderful warm summer nights. We ate grapes and berries. Fortunately, there was no rain.

Félix Goldschmidt had discovered where we were and came one night to bring us prayer books so that we could spend the holidays properly. On the Holy Day, he walked six kilometers to the edge of the vineyard, where he blew his shofar (ram's horn), to the great bewilderment of the workers. Of course, they had no idea why this little bearded, bespectacled man was blowing his horn. The sound of the shofar is part of the holiday ritual, which was important to my father and to Félix.

Alexandra

Officially, we had disappeared, and nobody but the Morissé family knew where we were. The rumors were flying. Every night we heard from the Morissé children, Jeanine and her brothers, what the rumors were. An airplane had landed in the field next to Les Troènes and had picked us up and taken us away. We had been arrested. We had been executed and our bodies removed. The Morissé family had a good time with these wild speculations. They always kept straight faces and didn't say anything.

There was a neighbor of the Morissé farm whom we didn't trust. He was a bachelor in his early forties who lived with his mother.

He was small and wiry. He looked like a caricature of a Frenchman, with dark, straight hair and a big nose and a little mustache. He was terribly chatty. That's why we didn't want him to know where we were, but he was so chatty and nosey that he found out. He heard us at night. But he kept his mouth shut and said nothing. He added to the rumors, and we later learned that he knew exactly where we were, but he didn't give us up. Ernest was his name.

At one point the grapes had to be harvested, and the farmer needed our shed for a few days. We had to move into a hay barn. They had hollowed out the top of the hayloft, where the straw was in bundles. The center of the straw was emptied out, and we had to climb up a long ladder to get into our nest and close the hay entrance behind us. At night we could go out, but the festivities lasted late at harvest time, so we didn't get out for very long.

The hay barn was also a meeting place for lovers. We didn't get to watch because we were enclosed and had no way of looking down. We were, however, auditory witnesses to a lot of hanky panky, and of course we knew most of these people, and therefore we also knew their voices. It was quite an education. I was quite young, and it was an earful. We just pretended that it wasn't happening, because we couldn't afford to giggle or to make ourselves known. Jeanine, of course, knew that we were there, but one of her hottest suitors somehow got her in there and pressed her, not for sex or anything like that – but to propose to her. The proposal was so rough and demanding.

"I want to marry you! I have to marry you! Don't say no to me!" It was very, very funny. It was really hard not to laugh. And, of course, Jeanine knew that we were listening to all of this. It must have been very hard for her, too. Eventually we could go back into our vineyard.

During all this time that we were in the Morissé vineyard, Goldschmidt was making false papers for us, so that we could escape from France to Switzerland. Our village mayor, Monsieur Morève, was with us in spirit, mind and heart.

Goldschmidt went to see the mayor shortly after we had disappeared into the vineyard, and asked, "Do you need any volunteer work done in the office?" And the mayor looked at him somewhat strangely.

Goldschmidt explained, "Yes, you know I have these evening hours, after eight in the evening, when I have nothing to do, and if you have some paperwork that I could learn to do, I would be very happy to occupy my time in the office." He then winked at the mayor.

The mayor winked back and replied, "Yes, I think I would like that very much," and then gave Goldschmidt the paperwork and stamps that Goldschmidt needed to make fake French identity cards for seven people. When they were ready, Goldschmidt declared to the mayor that he didn't have anything else to do.

Eva

During the day, we were not allowed to move. The door was made of wooden slats, which we covered with potato sacks that were given to us by Mr. Morissé. There were also sacks on the floor. We had a bucket with a lid but tried our best to wait until nightfall. For Grofa this was impossible, and when she had to use the pail, some of us crept to the top to give her privacy, and the rest of us turned our backs.

At night, we walked quietly in the vineyard. We each had our own tasks. My mother and I would go to the farmer's well. It had a little tower on top as a safeguard against animals or children falling in. The opening on top was a little bigger than the circumference of a bucket, and the rest was closed, going upwards to a point. We let the bucket down and poured the water into a trough. Here we washed the dirty clothes and hung them up to dry where they could not be seen.

The well was about 500 meters from the road, and when cars came by with their bright lights, my mother and I circled its little tower to keep out of sight. We were always afraid that they were deportation vehicles. The Germans would pull people out of their houses only at night, because the village people were so hostile towards them that they were afraid someone would shoot them or throw things at them during the day. They would drive around in ordinary vehicles in order to avoid attracting attention. We were also afraid that Minouche, our cat, would betray us. She had discovered where we were hiding, and we worried that people might follow her to us.

Eventually Mr. Morissé came to tell us that someone had seen us and that the Germans would come looking for us with dogs. If we were found in his vineyard, he and his family would also be deported. After three weeks in the vineyard hut, we had to leave.

Current shed in the vineyard, similar to the
2 x 2 meter shed in which the family hid for 3 weeks

Henri and Thérèse Morissé

Chapter Eleven
Lyon 1942

Lyon is known as the gastronomic center of the world; however, from 1942 to 1944, it had a very different reputation. Two famous men, one heroic and one notorious, were headquartered in Lyon. Klaus Barbie, also known as the "Butcher of Lyon," was one of the most heinous Nazis. Jean Moulin was one of the most famous resistance fighters.

Beginning in November 1942, when Germany decreed that there would no longer be a free zone, Klaus Barbie became the head of Nazi Germany's secret police in Lyon. He was responsible for sending seventy-five hundred French Jews and French resistance fighters to concentration camps and ordered the execution of another four thousand prisoners. His determination to kill every Jew in France led to one of the most tragic and horrific events in French history.

In 1944, there existed a Jewish children's home in the tiny, isolated village of Izieu, not far from Lyon. A former farmhouse, it seemed like the ideal spot to hide forty-one children ages three to seventeen who had no parents left to care for them. On April 6, Barbie sent a telegram to the Gestapo headquarters announcing that he had captured all forty-one children and ten staff and would be transferring them to the Montluc prison in Lyon. One week later, the children and most of their caretakers were deported to Auschwitz concentration camp, where only one adult survived.[17]

Lyon was also the headquarters of the French resistance movement. General Charles De Gaulle gave Jean Moulin the mission to unify the separate resistance movements into one coordinated group, the National Council of the Resistance. The two men's courses collided on June 21, 1943, when Moulin was captured and then personally interrogated and tortured by Barbie in Montluc prison.

Following the signing of the armistice in June 1940, the Montluc prison increasingly served the Vichy regime. The prisoners were first comprised of communists, anarchists, and resistance fighters with the gradual addition of Jews. Following the invasion of southern France, on November 11th, 1942, the German army requisitioned Montluc prison and had fully taken control by February 1943. From then until August 1944, it served as an interrogation center and holding facility for resistance fighters and Jews who were then sent to concentration camps. It is estimated that over 10,000 men, women, and children were imprisoned at Montluc. Over 900 Jews and resistance fighters were murdered within its walls, many after being tortured, and another 6,000 were sent to be murdered in concentration camps.[18]

The Butcher of Lyon returned to Germany in August 1944. Three years later, with full knowledge that he was a war criminal, the U.S. Army Counter-Intelligence Corps (CIC) recruited him to work for their organization. In 1949, the French government requested that the U.S. extradite Barbie from American officials. However, the CIC, determining that it was too risky to turn him over to the French, instead helped Barbie to escape to Bolivia, where he resettled with his family under the assumed name Klaus Altmann.

He was eventually captured by Nazi hunters and returned to France in 1983, where he was tried and eventually found guilty in 1987. He served the rest of his life in prison, beginning with a brief imprisonment at Montluc for symbolic purposes.

Plans were underway for the Kroch family to flee to Lyon. Unbeknownst to them, they were about to enter the "Butcher's Den."[19]

Aerial view of the National Memorial Prison at Montluc, Lyon, present day

Photo by juillet 1975© Arch. Dép. Rhône 4571 W 6

Judith

Now that we had our false French identity cards, we could take a train to Lyon without fearing the authorities. At least that is what we thought. In Lyon there were organizations that, for a hefty fee, smuggled French refugees across the Swiss border. Many Jews fled there to save their lives because Switzerland had remained neutral in both world wars and had not been invaded by the Germans.

We planned how to leave the vineyard hut. Félix brought us clothes from our house. We put on everything we had, one piece on top of the other, to avoid taking any luggage. Then he hired a small van, with benches on both sides. When the car stopped close to our vineyard, to which Félix had directed the driver, we hopped in, laughing, as if we had just made an innocent trip to the vineyard. We didn't want to be seen driving through the village, and we didn't want the taxi driver to know that we didn't want to be seen. It was important that the driver not become suspicious. So, Papa had devised a plan that he was going to light a cigarette just before entering the village and drop his entire box of matches on the floor of the taxi. When we entered the village, my father dropped the box of matches on the floor of the van, and we all bent down to pick them up. With all of us ducking simultaneously, the van looked empty from the outside.

Eva

We arrived in Lyon by train and went to the hotel that had been suggested to us. As we handed our documents to the hotel manager, I noticed him looking at them for longer than necessary. He called a member of the staff and passed the papers to him, which was normal. But I noticed a glance between the two men that made me uncomfortable.

We took our luggage to our rooms, and then went outside to find something to eat. As soon as I could, I turned to my father and said, "Papa, we have to get away from that hotel. I saw the way the manager looked at the other man. Something is wrong. He is calling the police."

And my father became furious. He screamed at me in front of everyone, "Don't cause panic. You are just causing panic. There is nothing wrong with our papers. Our papers are in order!"

105

When we returned to the hotel, my father announced, "We are leaving for Switzerland early tomorrow morning." But at six in the morning, there was the sound of a pencil tapping against our door. "Open, police."

Alexandra

Papa quickly gave instructions, "They are arresting us. If they don't arrest all of us, stay here. Goldschmidt is coming. Wait here."

They had immediately figured out that our identity papers were false. They arrested all the family except Grofa and me, because Grofa was over sixty, and I was under sixteen. According to the laws of Lyon, you could arrest a Jew if he or she was under sixty or over sixteen. So Grofa and I stayed in our hotel room, waiting for Goldschmidt. But before Goldschmidt arrived, the police came back, the same two policemen, one tall and dark, and one short and blond. And they arrested me. Why they could now arrest me, nobody explained to me. Grofa stayed and waited for Goldschmidt, who did come and did pick her up, and put her safely in a family in Vichy.

They took me away. I was quite frightened – not because they took me away, but because they took me away alone. I wouldn't have been half as frightened if I had been with my family. So, I tried to get them to tell me where they were taking me, and where they had taken my family. The short blond one, who seemed to be the boss, was also very mean, and he said, "You'll see. You'll see. You'll find out." And the tall one said nothing. They were French collaborators, the ones that worked for the Vichy government and collaborated with the Germans against the French. The shorter one had a ring with a swastika on it. I will never forget that hand.

And then something funny happened. They still hadn't told me where they were taking me, and I was still frightened. They took me to a trolley car. The little blond one asked me whether I had money for the fare. And I had to give him my twenty sous. That made me laugh. I actually laughed.

I said, "Yes I do!" and I gave it to him. And while he was buying the three tickets, the tall one just barely turned his head down toward me and whispered, "We take you to the same place." I have never forgotten that kindness. So then I was all right. They did take me to the same place, which was the prison in Lyon.[20]

Judith

The men were housed in cells with barred windows opening into a courtyard. The women had a room on the upper floor, but were not locked in. We were permitted to walk in the courtyard and look up at the men. Apart from the other Jews (few of them we had time to get to know, since they were so quickly deported), there were gypsies, foreigners without valid identification papers, and prostitutes. There were also some regular customers in this jail. One day an old, homeless woman walked up to a certain mattress and chased away the woman who had been lying there.

"This is my place," she said. It appeared that she had herself arrested from time to time so that she didn't always have to sleep outside on the pavement. The mattresses were rough sacks filled with dry corn stalks. During the day, they were propped up against the wall and were quiescent. As soon as they were put on the floor, they came to life. They were full of generations of bedbugs that were never short of nourishment. At first, we went hunting for them hopefully. But we soon realized that we would never win the battle except perhaps by burning down the jail.

In the morning, there was something indefinable to drink accompanied by a slice of bread. In the afternoon, we were given a thin saltwater soup with a few pieces of potato floating in it.

In the evening, when the names of fellow Jewish prisoners were called out for their departure towards an uncertain future, we were overcome by dread. What we feared most was that our family might be separated. While we were together, we believed we could endure anything. We had only a little inkling of the fate that awaited those who set out on their journey every evening. We learned more after the war. We did know that they would be sent to the Drancy camp and then to a concentration camp. We were afraid to be sent to a concentration camp. But we didn't know what happened to people once they arrived at the concentration camp, except that they would have to work hard. We didn't know until later that they would be gassed and burned. Our strength was that we were together. That was why we were so frightened every time they called the list.

When darkness came, Mutti, Eva, Alexandra, and I positioned ourselves in front of the men's windows and sang in harmony with Peter and Papa Fritz. We improvised on the melodies of the Schubert Trout Quintet. Mutti had also taught us old German chorales like "We Stand to Pray before God, the Just." We also sang our own melodic inventions in the style of Negro spirituals. It was sad and often moving, even for the other inmates.

One night, British planes came and dropped bombs. Instead of hiding, we ran into the courtyard and celebrated until morning. It was good to see that something was being done against the enemy.

Alexandra

To sleep, we had wooden bedsteads off the ground with straw mats, and that was it, no sheets or pillows. On the gray, dirty, masonry walls were strange rings about four to seven inches in diameter. For a while we couldn't imagine what they were. After the first night or two, we knew what they were. They were bedbugs that lived in our mattresses, and occasionally went out for a walk, and for some reason, they walked in circles. There would be several of them, in a circle. When somebody saw them, they would take a shoe and go "Plop, plop, plop, plop, plop." And that left a circle of dead bed bugs on the wall.

I fell madly in love with a young Spaniard, who was arrested because he was an illegal immigrant from Spain. He had a beautiful voice and sang beautiful Spanish songs. One day they brought in a young man with reddish-blond hair, and ears that were like teapot handles sticking out. They put him in the isolation cell. We were quite mystified because we had seen murderers and all kinds of criminals among us, and no one had been put in the isolation cell. This young man, it turned out, was a Maquisard (member of a rural guerrilla band of French Resistance fighters). He had been caught sending messages to England on a transmitter. That was, of course, the biggest crime you could commit. He was a spy for the Resistance.

The same day that he was caught, a woman was also caught, and charged with prostitution. It turned out, we found out later, that she was his contact from the resistance group. Because prostitutes didn't stay very long in jail, she could leave after she had made plans with him on how to get him out. The irony of it was that even though he was kept in the isolation cell, he was allowed out with the women! He wasn't allowed out at the same time as the other men. So we had contact with him, and he could talk with this alleged prostitute, who was his contact from outside until she was released. Later we heard that he had escaped. That was after we had already left.

While we were there, Goldschmidt, our benefactor, feverishly bribed his way from the jail officials up to the highest authorities of the Department du Rhone, to have us freed. It took time and money. He had time, but he didn't have money. So, he had to get the money. There were Jews in France, wealthy Jews, who liberally distributed money if they knew it was going to the right cause. Goldschmidt was a religious Jew who knew a lot of people. My father and Goldschmidt had planned so many things in advance. Goldschmidt knew exactly what to do.

Eva

The women were in a tremendous room, and on the floor were mattresses filled with dry maize leaves, which don't rot as quickly as straw. We sat on the mattresses to eat. They were filthy: soup, tears and who knows what. When you shook the mattresses, it made the maize leaves swell up, and that helped dry them.

Every night the prostitutes were brought in, and also people from other prisons and police stations. It was a depot, a short-term prison before sentencing. The prostitutes warmed my heart. Not all of them, of course, but some brought with them an attitude of helpfulness and generosity. I remember shivering with cold on my horrible mattress and being covered with my thin summer coat. Sometimes one of them would sleep next to me on my mattress, and we would cover ourselves with both of our coats, one over our feet and legs, and the other one over the top half of us. Some of them shared their food with me.

And this is how I met the hairdresser. She was brought in with the prostitutes, but there was something different about her. When she told me that she was a hairdresser, I asked her to do my hair for me, and she hesitantly agreed. I soon realized that she knew nothing about fixing hair. When I asked if I could help her in any way, she confided that she had been carrying messages for members of the Resistance, and that there were four such people in the prison at that moment. But she did not dare get in touch with them in case she was being watched.

The four men called themselves Athos, Porthos, and Aramis after the famous musketeers, and there was also D'Artagnan, the leader, who was in solitary confinement because he had been caught sending radio signals to the British. The special Nazi vehicle that intercepted such signals had stopped outside his door. He was sitting with his back to the door but heard it, and quickly signaled "Police, police" to the British because he knew their radio signals were being intercepted by the Nazis. The British then stopped using this line of contact. By sending this warning to the British, D'Artagnan had risked his life. And for this he was captured.

There was room for sixteen men to a cell, and they housed twenty. The prison was several stories high and was built around a big, high, rectangular courtyard. Between the prison and the street was a deep trench. A toilet for women was at the courtyard level, and the women were at liberty to walk around the courtyard, whereas the men had to remain in their cells. The women were able to look and speak through the barred windows of the men's cells. The only window that was open to the street, though barred, was the toilet window.

Athos gave me messages written on pieces of paper, which I folded into little balls. Then I went to the toilet, climbed on the toilet rim, and did my best to throw the folded notes out through the gaps of the bars, across the two-meter-wide trench, and again through the bars of the barrier that protected the passersby from falling into the trench. With time I succeeded in getting more of these notes across and into the street, where they lay. I don't know if anyone ever read them, and if any action was taken because of them. I often asked myself how it was possible that nobody ever asked questions about the notes. Some must surely have been picked up by informers or guards. They could easily have posted a female guard to watch us. Today I believe that only a minority of the police were pro-German, and I know that some of the guards were in the Resistance.

People were brought to our prison from other prisons and were held there to be deported at midnight. The general population of Lyon was not supposed to know this. The people in charge were French policemen who worked for the Germans. They wore swastika rings. They were Nazis, and always in some sense on the defensive. Some may have had a guilty conscience because, perhaps, they had reported someone to the police. At least, this is what I told myself the day I was called for interrogation.

Every morning between ten and twelve, people were called by name and stood in a line in the corridor, waiting to be interrogated. One at a time they were called into a large room. Gras and Vernieux, the two French Nazis, were there with their swastika rings. Gras was very big; Vernieux was smaller and slighter. I know that Vernieux was murdered later by the Resistance. The person who had been interrogated always came out of the room in a terrible state, beaten, holding their stomachs, their kidneys.

My brother was before me in line. We heard the groaning through the door. They beat him on his kidneys with their truncheons again and again. Peter could control himself. He did not scream, but we heard the screaming of his inquisitors.

"We'll teach you not to laugh!" When Peter was afraid or furious or in turmoil, he would grimace, and it was like a mask, as if he were grinning. And he made this grimace, certainly not on purpose, and they kept beating him until he collapsed. Then they let him out. He dragged himself out. He suffered from kidney trouble the rest of his life.

And then I went in. It was as follows: I had things to hide. I knew things that were happening in this prison. I knew things about the prisoners, about D'Artignan and his Musketeers and the hairdresser and others. I did not dare to be interrogated. I also knew something about myself; I knew that when they asked me something that I could answer without difficulty, I would answer quickly. And if I had to think about it, or was hiding something, I'd answer slowly, and then they'd know what questions to concentrate on.

I was wearing my summer coat, and one of the buttons had come off. I thought, "I must do something so that they won't know when I lie or when I tell the truth. If I know the answer immediately, for

instance, if they ask, 'How old are you?' I'll think as follows in order
to slow myself down, "My button has come off. I have it in my pocket.
I must sew it on. It isn't nice without a button." I told myself, "These
four sentences you will say in your head and then you will give your
date of birth. Then you will have a time span in which to think in case
you don't want to give the right answer."

They asked many questions, and I answered them all in this way,
slowly, quietly, and without showing fear. I did not smile or grin with
fear, like my brother. I can thank my father for that. I would not have been
allowed to grin when he was angry with me. So, even my father being
angry with me had its good aspect. Everything has a good aspect.

I sat there and answered every question in this way, and then
he asked, "When were you born?"

I replied, "On the 29th of April, 1932," and then corrected
myself, "1923."

He said, "You are not very sure about your age."

So I said, "But I don't look like a ten-year-old! I made a mistake
because I am agitated."

Then the big one, Gras, stood up and told Vernieux, "Shut the
windows!" Shutting the windows meant that the people in the street
should not hear my screams. This I knew. He took the stick, and
Vernieux went to shut the windows. The room was at least six by seven
meters. Along the narrower wall were two very big windows, which he
closed with wooden shutters and locked with an iron, horizontal bar.
There was one writing desk on the longer side, towards the middle of
the room. And behind it, at some distance from me, sat Gras.

He got up with his stick. I sat almost opposite the door by the
narrower wall. The door was close to the corner, about four meters
away from him and about four meters from the desk. Vernieux left,
and Gras approached me with the stick, and I thought, "If someone so
big beats a girl (I was so small and delicate looking), he must have a
guilty conscience. So, I'll do something innocent." When he got up, I
also got up. And when he approached me and lifted the hand with the
stick, I slowly walked towards him. He was still asking questions, and I
was still answering. But with every step he took towards me, I took one
towards him. After two meters, when I was standing a meter away from

him, I suddenly saw him smile.

The stick went down, and he said, "Get out of here!" He must have known that I was afraid, but that I was so innocent that I came towards him. That struck him as funny, and he let me go. He also let my sister Judith and mother go. They were just behind me. I am sure that my behavior saved them from damage to their health.

Félix Goldschmidt did what he could from the outside. He bribed and bribed. Every day, the deportation list arrived. The people on the list were sent to Auschwitz. And one day at 6 pm, we were called and brought to Gras. He gave us papers and said, "Go with this man." And a man led us out.

But to get out of the prison, we had to pass the whole line of people who stood there, waiting to be deported at midnight. I felt so bad, so terribly guilty that we were being freed. As we passed them, we gave each one our hands.

"We will meet again! We will meet again!" We knew and they knew that we would not meet again. I remember a mother and daughter who had been arrested and brought to the prison room where we slept. Whenever the mother wept, the daughter comforted her in Yiddish, "veyn nischt mame, veyn nisht." "Don't cry, Mother." And now they were standing in the line.

Judith

After a month in prison, we were released. Félix and Grofa were waiting for us at the prison entrance. Félix gave us fresh courage. His cheerful disposition and optimism influenced all of us. Only those who have ever been imprisoned can know the feeling of exhilaration upon suddenly being free.

We boarded a train from Lyon to Annonay, where we changed to go on by bus to Lalouvesc. The little community to which we were sent could be reached only by bus. It is in the department of Ardèche, on top of the mountain of the Massif Central at 1050 meters.

Eva

We were given two rooms in a Residence Forcée (forced residence). It was the condition of our freedom enforced by the state.

113

We had no money, so we begged for food from the farmers. They gave us cabbages that they didn't want to eat because they had been frozen. Only the middle was good, and we were afraid that our mother might throw away the outer leaves, so we washed the outer leaves in the snow and ate them raw on our way home, bringing our mother the tiny inner part of the cabbages, which she cooked. We also looked for chestnuts. The forests were full of them, and we roasted them, boiled them, or ate them raw. We ate a lot of cabbages and chestnuts.

The place itself was lovely. I have so many memories of Lalouvesc that my sister-in-law once said to me, years later, "It's a disgrace to have so many good memories of the war!" Weaving up the mountain were serpentine roads, and near the peak was a hollow and, in that hollow, lay the little village where we lived. We were surrounded by mountains. When you stood on the edge of the village, you saw the rising wall of the mountain behind you, and a heavy fence in front of you. Beyond the fence was a drop of 500 meters, which in the winter was usually filled with clouds. On a clear day I would look straight down and see the most beautiful trees, bare of leaves except for the fir trees; and farmsteads all covered with snow.

There were other Jewish families being kept in Lalouvesc, but we had nothing to do with them. We kept to ourselves because we never knew who might be an informer. We were all afraid of one another. We knew that it would soon be time to leave. Offering our family "freedom" in this village was only a way of ensuring that the officials could "collect" us when the time came for us to be arrested.

Alexandra

My father immediately figured out what was going on.

"This is no good. They're just filling up this village until they have a truckload full of Jews. Then one night they're going to pick us up and take us away, and nobody will know the difference."

This was later confirmed by the fact that the mayor of this village was a violent antisemite, and pro-Nazi. The police under his command were sort of in between. They didn't quite know how to handle this. The mayor, after all, was their boss. So immediately Papa planned how we could get out.

Fortunately, I already had this crooked back, which was diagnosed when I was twelve. The curvature (scoliosis) had been discovered at Les Troènes in Mézières by my sister Eva. So, this bad back was part of the saving grace because my mother took me to the local doctor, who looked at my back.

"This child needs help," he said, and wrote a certificate that declared that my mother and I needed to go to Lyon to get special help for my back. Since a fifteen-year-old girl couldn't travel alone, my mother and I received traveling passes to go to Lyon. There we had contacts (again through Goldschmidt) with people who made it their business to both finance and find ways to get Jews out of France into Switzerland.

In Lyon, Mutti had found the right kind of smuggling operation that would eventually bring us out of France. In peacetime, these enterprises would smuggle stolen goods or jewels. During this war, they had human merchandise to smuggle out, which brought in at least as much money, and kept them quite busy. Once Mutti secured the right smuggling ring and found out how much it cost, my father went to Félix Goldschmidt again. Through Félix, my father obtained a loan from a very wealthy and orthodox Jew who lived in Lyon. This man had decided to help as many Jews as he could. He gave my father the amount of money we needed without security, since he didn't know who would make it and who would not. Eventually, he had sent his family away when the Germans had taken over Lyon and started arresting the French Jews. But he still had money to give away, so he stayed. After the war we found out he didn't make it out, but his family did survive.

Planning our escape was quite a complicated organization. On one particular day, a Friday afternoon, my father went with my sisters to the doctor in Lalouvesc. The doctor sympathized with their plight. He diagnosed Eva with having a blockage in her nose, a congenital disorder that needed surgery urgently. He diagnosed Judith with having one hip a quarter of an inch higher than the other. I know now that 80 percent of the female population in the world suffers from this condition. He certified her need for immediate attention by a specialist. With these medical certificates, on that Friday afternoon, my brother went with one of my sisters to the Commissariat de Police, and my father went with the other sister to the mayor's office. You had to have a certificate from either one of these two places in order to travel. We planned the timing so that these two organizations couldn't speak to each other, as we didn't want the authorities to notice that the whole family was traveling at the same time.

It was arranged that Grofa would take a train from Vichy, where she had been staying with a family, ostensibly to join us in Lalouvesc. But, in fact, the train had to take her through Lyon, and we were going to intercept her there. She knew that. So, it was planned that the four of them would take the bus to Lyon the next morning bright and early, armed with their medical certificates.

Judith

Our last night in Lalouvesc, we spent preparing food for the journey. We still had a little flour that we didn't want to leave behind. Everything edible left in the house was mixed into dough, which was baked into flat loaves. Towards the morning, the firewood for the oven ran out, so we burnt first the coat hangers, then the clothes pins and, in the end, an old chair. Satisfied, but not without trepidation, we set out for Lyon early Saturday morning.

After our arrival in Lyon for the second time, we went to a hotel where guests were not asked to register with the police. No sooner had we sat down in our little room than a wall began to lean towards us. We cried out in horror. The wall was slowly, slowly falling in our direction. There was no escape. And then the wall miraculously straightened back up. First, we had to get over the shock. But then we realized that our room, like many others perhaps in this hotel, had double walls behind which people or goods could be concealed. Most likely there were not only refugees like us in the hotel, but criminals as well. Feeling very uneasy, we lay down on top of our beds, fully dressed. We could hardly sleep. The trip to Switzerland was to start in the morning.

The arrangement was that a moving van would drive us up to the border. From there we would have to cross on foot to Switzerland. We were requested to arrive at the moving company singly or in small groups of not more than three or four, and we were warned to check if anyone was following us. Though we were given directions, we were not allowed to write down the address.

Mutti, together with Grofa, Papa, and Alexandra, started out. Peter, Eva, and I waited for a quarter of an hour before going to the tramway that was to take us to our destination. On the way, we were followed by three men who kept looking at us. We pretended not to see them. However, when they boarded the same tram as we did, we began to worry. At the next stop, we got off to see if they would stay in the tram, in which case we would be rid of them. But that didn't happen. Instead, they got up quickly and stayed close to us.

We did not know the city and had to stay reasonably close to the tram tracks in order to find our way. Nevertheless, we held a quick conference and decided to risk a small detour through some side streets. We decided that Peter would go alone, and Eva and I would take another route, and then we would all meet at the tram stop. In a strange city, this was a daring plan, since we had to be at the moving firm by a certain time. "Dear God, save us from informers!" We could not get rid of them. They stuck to us like chewing gum. I felt more than fear. I felt panic. "Now it's all over! Everything was for nothing," These men were trailing us to find out where we were heading and then would arrest us. Where could we turn for help?

After almost getting lost several times, we finally ended up near the moving company. We stopped and waited to see where the men would go now. As soon as we saw the building, they went straight to the gate and vanished inside. We were standing and watching carefully, ready to bolt, when Papa Fritz appeared and motioned us to come in. The men we had so greatly feared were also Jewish refugees, who had followed us because they were not sure of the way. It never occurred to them that they had frightened us almost to death. They had been much impressed by our technique of shaking off informers.

After all this excitement, our nerves were so tightly stretched that we were unable to appreciate the comical side of the story. The stress of constant, terrible fear had been with us day after day. Now I felt depressed. It is true that in Mézières-en-Brenne, we had a wonderful time with the Goldschmidts, our parents and siblings and our brave Grofa, in spite of hunger, in spite of the war. In Lalouvesc, we were still cheerful. We always found something beautiful, enjoyed nature, laughed and sang. That was how our parents strengthened our confidence. So far, we had been lucky. But luck can also run out. Would we succeed?

Two large moving vans loaded with furniture were parked in the garage. With hardly enough time to go to the bathroom, we had to climb deep inside the truck. We traveled that way for several hours, without fresh air and unable to move. The truck made several stops; German soldiers opened the doors, shone their flashlights all over the furniture, and shut the door again. Everything was in order. We could go on.

Alexandra

The total group of fifteen of us were put inside a furniture van, which had no windows. We were all pushed way back behind the furniture, where we sat on crates or benches. To the outside world, there were layers of mattresses, beds, and pianos so that no one could see us. We were able to communicate with the driver in the cab. When he spoke loudly, we could hear him. He could hear us, too, if we spoke loudly. So, it was agreed that if he knocked on the panel between us, we would be quiet. At one point we heard a knock on the panel, so we all became very quiet. We heard a conversation between the truck driver and another man. The other man, from what we could hear, was a French policeman on his bicycle. The truck driver invited him in the cab, and he hung his bicycle on the furniture outside our van. For quite a stretch, we had a policeman in our van!

Chapter Twelve
Switzerland, December 1942

Switzerland maintained a position of armed neutrality during World War II. Consequently, this country bordering Germany, Italy, and France was poised to be a safe haven for refugees fleeing persecution from Nazis. However, various policies and laws were enacted by the Swiss government that served to block access to Jews. Between 1933 and 1944, asylum for refugees could be granted only to those under personal threat due to political activities, and this did not include threats due to race, religion, or ethnicity.

Even under these restrictions, some Jews did make it through and were accepted into refugee camps. There were several reasons why this happened. Individual cantons (member states) interpreted the laws differently, and some were more lenient than others in accepting Jews. Also, public sentiment among the Swiss was largely supportive of the Jewish plight.

Under threat of punishment, smugglers continued to bring Jewish refugees over the border. They were well paid and willing to take the risk. There is ample evidence that the Swiss government did collaborate with German authorities in restricting Jewish immigration. It was the chief of Swiss Police, Heinrich Rothmund, who proposed to the Germans that "J" be affixed to the passports of Jews in order to better identify them.

On August 13, Mr. Rothmund explained that "In the future, more civilian refugees must therefore be refused entry, even if this might result in serious consequences for them (threat to life and limb)." His rationale was that the country was struggling with limited supplies of food and found the task of housing the refugees and caring for them to be daunting. This decree also stipulated that "Money or valuables that were used or intended for use as payment" were to be confiscated from the Jewish refugees attempting to cross into Switzerland. These measures reflected the antisemitic position underscoring these policies.[21]

Despite these new orders, Jewish refugees continued to enter

Switzerland and were sent to detention camps because it was so difficult to control the borders and to exert control over individual jurisdictions. The number of Jews allowed entry and refused entry are very hard to calculate. Some estimates suggest that thirty thousand Jews seeking asylum were admitted, and the same amount were refused entry.[22]

As the Kroch family embarked on the last stretch of their escape, they were unaware of the great odds against their successful flight to Switzerland. At each step of their treacherous journey, they were at great risk of being apprehended and killed. The Krochs had entrusted their lives to nameless smugglers who provided their services for part of their escape. Did they know that they would be left to their own devices when they reached the summit? Were they forewarned by their handlers that they would have to navigate the perilous route down the Alps into Switzerland on their own? Had they any inkling that the Swiss guards were refusing entry to many of the Jews who had made it to the border?

Judith: Ascent

As it grew dark, we reached a village in the French Alps where we unloaded. It was so cold in December that the night was glistening. We were given a glass of hot cocoa. Other smugglers took charge of us. They explained that we would have to follow a goat track that was very narrow and steep. The better-known path to the border was carefully watched by German military patrols, and we had to remain undetected. Some sugar cubes were distributed (such luxury!) to give us energy for the arduous and dangerous climb.

The ascent began. At first, it was bearable, for it warmed us up, but soon the multiple layers of clothing, which we wore to avoid carrying luggage, became cumbersome. On the western side of the mountain where we were climbing, there was no snow, but the road was icy. We had to test the ground very carefully before taking a step so as not to slip. After a while, the guide signaled that we should lie down, press ourselves as close as possible to the rock face, and stay perfectly still. A German border patrol passed on the path above us. We could hear them talking. My heartbeat was so loud and strong that I feared it would betray us. Each of us said a silent prayer: "Please let us remain undetected." After long minutes, stiff with cold and fear, we got up and climbed further.

Grofa was about the age I am now: in her sixties. She was stout, had a congenital heart defect, and was short of breath. Peter took loving care of her, supporting her heavy body. We girls had relieved her of the few belongings without which she could not possibly live – for instance, her hairbrush, her toiletries, and pictures she had brought from Germany. I didn't think it was ridiculous. Those things meant more to her than anyone can imagine. Even for the rest of us, the going was hard in our poor shoes with wooden soles, which were in no way suitable for mountain climbing. We were panting; overtaxed, overtired, but wide awake, hearts pounding, shivering and perspiring at the same time. But no one dared to stop.

Our group of fifteen was a long time scrambling up the mountain. Time was an important factor. We had to get to the top ridge before dawn. "Allez, allez, faster!" We made one last, mighty effort. Without looking up or down, we clambered on, meter after meter. Seven hours later, inappropriately dressed and still greatly fearing for our lives, we finally reached our goal: the Col du Cou: 1,921 meters high into the French Alps. As the sun rose, Switzerland, all white, lay before us. The slope facing east was completely covered with snow, so that the first of the group to attempt the descent sank deep into white powder.

Eva: Ascent

We began the climb on foot. It was pitch dark, and the guides walked ahead of us as we followed them, one behind the other. I remember that I suddenly slipped. A big hand grabbed me by the coat and pulled me up, and a voice said softly, "If you fall here, you don't have to walk to Switzerland. It's five hundred meters down." So, somebody saved my life, and it was so dark that I never knew who it was.

At another point during the night while we were climbing, Grofa was behind me, and I could hear her panting and I said, "Grofalein, is it terribly hard for you? Should we rest for a little while?"

And she replied, "Don't you dare stop. Either I walk with you or I lie down here and die, and you will be intelligent enough to leave me here!" She was heroic. People are suddenly heroes at times when you don't expect it. We had a grandmother in her sixties who seemed ancient to us. And she was the one to say, "Leave me – either I die, or I succeed. You make sure that you save yourselves."

We got to the top as the day dawned, and in front of us, in a wide descent, was a gigantic expanse of snow.

Alexandra: Descent

When we reached the top, the smugglers were paid the last installment of their fee, and they then informed us that they would not accompany us into Switzerland. We stood on top of this mountain ridge, which was only a foot wide at the crest. Behind us was France, and in front of us was Switzerland. The Swiss side was covered with snow and ice, but we had to get down. First, we celebrated; we laughed, we sang, we ate whatever sandwiches we still had in our possession, and then we started our descent.

Peter was the first one to step onto Swiss soil. He sat on his behind because his foot had no way to hold his weight on that icy, snowy surface.

He pulled himself back to French soil. "We can't do it. We can't walk down there."

"I'll show you how to do it!" Grofa declared. She gathered her skirts, sat on her behind, and started schussing down on her bottom. We all followed her. We were wearing all the clothes that we owned. I was wearing three pairs of panties, and a petticoat and a skirt, a slip and a dress, a coat and two pairs of thick stockings, plus a pair of socks. In addition, I wore this horrible corset that had just been made for my crooked back. We sat on our behinds, and we just schussed down. When I say schussed, I mean we controlled our slipping with our elbows.

There were no trees, but big rocks stuck out, and we had to circumnavigate the boulders. In places it was very steep, and in those places, we tried to go diagonally so as not to go so steeply.

Eva: Descent

All of us had torn stockings and clothes and bleeding scratches, red, frozen legs, and wounds on our buttocks. Some of the snow was hard ice, and there were also jagged bits of rock just under the surface. We didn't just go smoothly downwards, as it had looked from the tops. Along the way were sudden drops and rises. My grandmother did not once cry out in pain. I respected her so. She was the one to lead the way down the mountain. No long debate, no hesitation. It had to be "Go!"

Alexandra

It took us well past midday to get down. It was in the afternoon when we found a road. We had seen a village in the distance, and that's where we aimed. As we entered the village, we walked toward the border post, and were greeted by Swiss border guards who counted us.

"There are still two missing," one guard pointed out.

"How do you know?" we asked.

So, he explained, "In the morning we count the dots on the ice. And at night before it gets dark, we have to find you all, because otherwise it's too cold in the mountains at night. You might freeze to death. So, we have to hunt down the last dot. We are two short right now."

Eva

At the bottom, Swiss soldiers were waiting for us. They were rough and unfriendly and took us to a large room. The expressions on the faces of the refugees around me, and probably mine as well, were a mixture of fatigue, hope, apprehension, and uncertainty. "What will happen next?" We didn't get anything to eat or drink. The Swiss soldiers were so unpleasant that we became afraid. The sergeant asked us how old we were, so we each gave our age.

He sent people in two directions and, pointing at the one group, said, "Those go away." In our group were people over sixty, everyone who had children fifteen or under, and all young people under twenty-five. All the members of our family belonged in this category.

I asked him what was going to happen to the others.

So, he told me, laughing, "Well, we are sending them back to France. They don't fit our norms. And those that have a big nose like this one" – and he made a gesture with his hand showing a big hooked nose, and then pointed to a young man – "I'll give him straight to Lieutenant Witwer, and he will be sent back to Germany."

That was our first welcome to Switzerland. No jubilations. We were sent to a Bex Les Bains, a children's home that was turned into a refugee camp.

Judith: Postscript

We had survived. While we were held in a refugee camp in Switzerland, we saw the end of the Second World War. The first witnesses of the horror arrived from Poland, Russia, and Germany. From survivors we heard of the unspeakable, unimaginable atrocities. We had been spared this terrible fate. Our entire family of seven people had escaped, alive. Everything that happened to us is small, unimportant, not worth the telling when compared with the experiences of those who lost whole families under the most dreadful conditions.

For almost forty years I have carried the memories of those days and kept them within myself. I wanted to give my children a carefree childhood. I didn't want them to be burdened with the story of their mother. I also knew that it would be difficult for me to describe fear without feeling it anew.

Alexandra, Judith, Eva, and Peter, 1950

Postscript

My mother often rejoiced in how lucky she was. Although she never brought up her family's survival as proof of her good fortune, I imagine that this was what drove her attitude. The survival of my mother and her family rested on so many factors, but ultimately their many rescuers and their careful planning would not have been enough to keep them alive had it not been for their many extraordinary windfalls of luck. Each one of those moments when someone came to their rescue, or something happened that saved them from mortal danger can only be attributed to a random, coincidental circumstance of astonishing good fortune.

There were millions of Jews and other victims of the Holocaust who did have the stamina, the rescuers to aid them, and had carefully planned their escape. The one missing ingredient was luck. It was ultimately tremendous luck that separated those who survived from those who perished.

Epilogue

With the end of World War II in September 1945, the Kroch family members were liberated from their refugee camps, whereupon they returned to the Hotel Commerce, their familiar "home" in Paris. Eventually they found their footing, enjoying prosperous and fulfilling lives in new countries. Lore and Fritz moved to Israel with Grofa, where they lived a comfortable life in Tel-Aviv.

Fritz died at age 84, and Lore and Grofa each lived to be 94. Before they became scattered around the world, the four Kroch children made a pact that they would each teach their children French as their first language. This would enable the cousins to communicate with each other when anticipated reunions would occur. And happily, this plan was successfully executed. My childhood included visits to Israel every few years to gather with my cousins and the rest of the Kroch clan at the Holy Land Hotel, which had been built by my Uncle Hans.

Kroch family reunion, Israel, 1965. L to r: Bottom row Ben and Celia (Alexandra) Dorothée and Bettina (Eva) Eri and Ayala and behind them Yoya (Peter); Middle row sitting: Alexandra, Eva with Frank on her lap, Grofa, Ellen (wife of Peter), Judith; Back row standing: Raphael (husband of Alexandra), Chai (Husband of Eva), Lore and Fritz, Peter, Moshe (husband of Judith), Shaul (son of Moshe), Amatsia and Michal (Judith)

Félix Goldschmidt: "Proud and Worthy"

On July 12, 1943, Félix's luck ran out. He was arrested by the Gestapo for creating false papers and sent to a prison in Chateauroux, where he was tortured, and later transferred to a prison in Limoges. In his cell was another prisoner, an agent of the FBI, who taught him how to jump from a moving train. In October 1943, Félix was condemned to death and sent to Drancy Deportation Camp. There he managed to write letters to his wife. His last letters read as a spiritual will and testament in the event that he never saw his wife and children again. These letters are included in the note section. [23]

In Drancy, he was housed in a barrack with fifty other men. Goldschmidt's group of prisoners adopted the motto: "Proud and Worthy," which they painted on the wall of their barracks. Félix was to be executed for being a resistance fighter, but since he was Jewish, he was sentenced to go to Auschwitz instead. He immediately began to plan his escape. Every night, he and forty-nine men under his tutelage practiced how to jump safely from a moving train.

The trains usually ran at night because the Germans didn't want the population living along the route to see a train of cattle cars filled with people. He knew that jumping from a train, even if he was killed in the attempt, was no worse than imprisonment in a concentration camp. On November 20, he and his fifty fellow inmates were loaded onto a cattle train with twelve hundred other Jews, bound for Auschwitz concentration camp. As the train passed through the Bar-le-Duc region, the prisoners in his car started leaping, one by one, and Goldschmidt was going to jump last. All but one man jumped. The last one refused. As they approached the border, Goldschmidt decided there was no time left. He needed to jump.

Goldschmidt jumped, rolled away from the tracks, and promptly fell into a ravine. A sapling stopped his fall. It became instantly clear that he had broken his leg and ankle in the fall, and that moving might result in his falling farther down the ravine. He needed to stay perfectly still to avoid plunging farther down into the ravine. He had aspirin in his pocket and took a number of them in order to sleep very soundly.

He woke up with the sun and saw that the ravine was about

two or three times deeper and realized at that moment that he would have been killed had he fallen any farther. He managed to grab a piece of the sapling, break it off, and use it as a crutch. He then climbed out and walked until he found a road that led in the direction of a village. He had just started along that road when he met a couple of girls who brought him to Gabriel and Simone Philbert, a family living in the village of Nancois-sur-Ornain. These brave people provided shelter, nursed him, and hid him for the next two months so that he could safely recuperate.

Goldschmidt was very anxious to have his wife and children know that he was alive in France. On the other hand, he didn't want to put them, the Philbert family, or himself in jeopardy. He couldn't just send a letter or send his address. So, he arranged that Mr. Philbert would write to Félix's nephew, René Klein, inviting him for a visit. In case the letter was to fall into the wrong hands, there was a safety catch. When René Klein arrived at the farm, Goldschmidt was not there to greet him. The plan was that Mr. Philbert would talk to René Klein, offer him a cigarette, and place an open book of matches in front of him. Inside the matchbook, Goldschmidt had written "Beatrice," (Batia) which was the name of his eldest child, and then dash, dash, dash, dash: spaces for his other four children. If the person in front of Mr. Philbert was indeed René Klein, then he would know the four names of Félix's children. René wrote in "Jules, Eve, Tili, and René," and a relieved Félix entered the room to greet his nephew.

Of the twelve hundred Jewish prisoners on his train, nine hundred fourteen were gassed upon arrival in Auschwitz. Twenty-two men and two women survived, and nineteen, including Félix, escaped. The Goldschmidt family lore is that Félix was the only Jew who survived the war because he was a Jew. All the non-Jewish resistance fighters were executed on the spot. However, since Félix was a Jew, he was sentenced instead to go to Auschwitz. He took the opportunity to escape, and so survived his death sentence.

Goldschmidt was reunited with his family, and they all escaped to Switzerland. But the stories of Félix's contribution to humanity continued. During their time as refugees in Switzerland, Félix and his wife, Marguerite, became directors of a children's home set up by the

Red Cross called Waldrössili, in Schwendibach, near the Lake of Thun.

After the war, Félix and Marguerite became the directors of the Versailles Children's Home in France. They became the surrogate parents to fifty orphaned Jewish children and adolescent survivors of concentration camps. Elie Wiesel was one of those children.

In 1953, Félix and Marguerite moved to Israel. Félix continued his humanitarian work, aiding Jewish refugees from other countries. He translated the Eichmann trial from German and Hebrew into French in 1961. Marguerite died in 1963; Félix passed away three years later.

Gabriel and Simone Philbert were awarded the title Righteous Among the Nations, the Yad Vashem award, on November 11, 2007.

Yael Vered wrote a book about Félix Goldschmidt. She started to write the book in 1980 (twenty-four years after Félix's death), during her stay in Paris, where she worked as ambassador of Israel to UNESCO, the United Nations Educational, Scientific and Cultural Organization. The book was published in Hebrew in 1999 and translated into French by Félix's son Jules Goldschmidt in 2006. The French title is Là où il n'y à pas d'hommes, tâche d'être un homme ("There where there are no men, try to be a man.") The preface was written by Elie Wiesel.

The Kroch family and members of the Goldschmidt family have remained friends to this day.

Group portrait of the younger boys in the Versaille Children's Home. René (Chmouel) Goldschmidt in the center with his friends, 1947
Courtesy of the United States Holocaust Memorial Museum

Versaille Children's Home. Inside the home's synagogue,
Félix reads to the children, 1947-49, Seine-et-Oise, France
Courtesy of the United States Holocaust Memorial Museum

Erna, the Governess

Before the war, as threats to Jews mounted, Erna took the Kroch family photographs and buried them in a box in her back yard. After the war, when she established that the Kroch family had survived, Erna dug up the pictures and tracked down the Krochs. She found that they were living in Paris and sent the photographs with this letter: "My Dear Mrs. Kroch, Since you have lost all your possessions, you now need these pictures of your children more than I do."

Our family kept in touch with Erna. Before the Berlin Wall came down, my grandmother sent her letters and money. In the early 1980s, my mother received a letter from Erna's sixteen-year-old granddaughter, Jana, requesting that they begin a correspondence. My mother had sent Erna Christmas cards every year since they had rediscovered each other.

Erna and her family still lived in the communist part of Germany. Against the advice of everyone, my parents decided to obtain visas in order to visit Erna and her family in Leipzig. Colleagues warned my father that it was dangerous for a physicist to travel to a communist country. But they did travel to East Germany and met Erna again, along with Jana and her father, who was Erna's son. My mother recalled that "They put on a big spread for us which was probably a month's worth of rations. I don't think they were actually rationed, but food was not plentiful."

Monique Boucheny from Le Paradis

Monique, the only child of Marceau, the French soldier who had rescued the Kroch women, remained a close friend of my mother throughout her life. When I was young, our family took a trip to Aulnay-la-Riviere to visit the Boucheny family. I remember meeting Mémé and Pépé, Monique and her husband, Touré, and their four children. Since then, I have reconnected with Marie-Hélène, one of Monique's daughters. We met up in Paris a few years ago. Marie-Hélène, who still lives in the small village of Aulnay-la-Rivère, shared with me some of the stories that her mother, Monique, recounted about her time with Alexandra during the war. For a short time after returning with her mother, sister, and grandmother to Paris, my mother attended school there. Her friend Monique was also attending a private school in Paris, since there were no schools in the small village where she lived. During that time, Monique remembered how much her friend Alexandra hated to wear the yellow star. And when they rode together on the bus to and from school, Monique, a non-Jew, would sit with her friend in the back of the bus, where the Jews were made to sit. This brave and poignant gesture of resistance on the part of Alexandra's childhood friend Monique may have been one of the factors that cemented their lifelong friendship.

Monique, Madeleine, and
Marceau Boucheny

Alexandra and Raphael visiting
Madeleine, (Marceau's daughter)
with her husband Touré in Le Paradis

Alexandra visiting Pépé at Le Paradis, 1953

Marie-Hélène, one of
Monique's daughters

Peter

After the war, Peter immigrated to Palestine. In 1948, he enlisted in the Palmach, the forerunner of the Israeli Army, and fought in the Israel War of Independence. He later became an officer. He continued his love of music and storytelling. Peter's loving and disarming personality brought joy to everyone in his orbit. He brought his wife, Ellen, and three children to upstate New York to live near us for two years in order to work with my father in developing an electronics firm while also studying mainframe computers at Cornell University. When he returned to his home in Haifa, he helped to found Elron, an electronics company in Haifa, a predecessor to Elbit, a giant Israeli company today.

Peter remained kosher and attended synagogue until he died. For Peter, as had been for Papa Fritz, upholding a religious life was not so much God's commandment as it was keeping Jewish traditions alive, and in doing so, keeping Jewish people united and alive.

Peter tragically died at age 58 from heart failure. He frequently spoke to them about his life during the Second World War, and he intended to write his memoir, but unfortunately passed away before achieving this goal. All we have left of his war experiences are the memories of his three sisters, and some stories he told his children over the Shabbat dinner table. Peter had three children, and now has seven grandchildren and three great-grandchildren.

*Peter and Ellen on
their wedding day,
1951*

Eva

Eva stayed in Paris, married a Frenchman, and had three children. Chai Heymann, her husband, died suddenly in 1968 at the age of forty-nine. He had been cranking his car to start it, and his heart stopped. Chai had not been a well man when he married Eva. His heart had been weakened by malaria. He was a Zionist and had instructed Eva that if he should die, he wanted her to move to Israel, which is exactly what she did. She had six grandchildren and four great-grandchildren.

Twenty years ago, a friend convinced Eva to dictate her life story in French, which was then translated into Hebrew and English. It is this memoir that provides her voice in this book. Eva's feeling that her father did not favor her was substantiated throughout her life. It was a fact that even I was aware of.

Our beautiful Eva suffered from severe osteoporosis, which left her unable to walk, and in constant pain. During her last few years, she was totally bedridden and dependent on nurses to tend to all her needs, yet until the end, her mind was totally sharp, and she was able to speak fluently in four languages. Throughout her life, Eva was a most positive, optimistic person with no trace of bitterness despite the many difficulties thrown in her path. Until her death on April 3, 2017, just shy of her ninety-fourth birthday, she maintained a wonderful sense of humor, enjoying the telling and retelling of her favorite jokes. She was a beautiful lady full of grace and dignity.

Eva and Chai on their wedding day, 1952

L to r in back Fritz, Lore; in front: Eva, Chai, Grofa

Judith

Judith moved to Israel and married an Israeli pioneer, Moshe Kashti, who helped to establish the Beit HaShita kibbutz. Judith was a devoted sister to Eva. When Eva, newly widowed, moved to Israel with her three young children, Judith welcomed them into her home. They lived together for 6 months until Eva regained her footing. Throughout their lives the two sisters remained very close. Judith was her lifeline for the last years of her life when Eva was totally bedridden, visiting her several times a week, providing love and companionship. I heard Judith remark that they were keeping each other alive. She had two children, seven grandchildren, and six great-grandchildren. Her spirit, mind, and body evoked a woman twenty years younger than her years. On her eightieth birthday, she took her children and grandchildren on a pilgrimage to Germany, retracing her life before the war, conducting a tour with herself as the guide. In 1993, she was inspired to write a book about her family and the war that shattered their lives. The book, "Running for Survival," is translated into four languages. Sections from her book, as well as face to face interviews, constitute her voice in this story. Judith died on October 9, 2019 at the age of ninety-four.

Judith and husband Moshe

Four Generations: Lore's first great-grandchild, baby Maya, with Lore's daughter Judith and granddaughter Michal

Alexandra and Raphael on their wedding day, 1950

Alexandra

My mother was living in Paris at the Hotel de Commerce, the same hotel the family had stayed in before the war, when on July 13, 1948, her father came home and announced to her and her sister Judith, "One of you has to go out on a date with Raphael Littauer tomorrow." That day just happened to be July 14, French Independence Day. Judith and my mother had already decided that they were not making any dates so that they could go out together, and paint the town red. For that reason, they declined the date. That was not an answer that their father would accept. Since Fritz explained that one of them was obligated to spend Independence Day with this blind date, they both decided to accompany Raphael.

Despite her reluctance, my mother and Raphael hit it off instantly, leaving Judith as the awkward third wheel. The long evening was spent dancing at nightclubs and culminated with my mother breaking the heel of her shoe and needing to be carried piggyback home by my father. It was love at first sight for both.

My father returned to London the next day, but the torch had been lit, and the flame continued across the English Channel. My father visited my mother several times before they were married in 1950.

My father often recounted his first glimpse of the Kroch family after the war. He had known that before the war this family was among the wealthiest in Leipzig, and now he was meeting them in a dingy hotel as they sat on their suitcases, joking around and happy to be together. His first impression of them, which never left him, was of a family that radiated pure joy despite having lost every vestige of material wealth. We heard him describe this moment many times. My father was offered a position in the physics department at Cornell University in Ithaca, New York, where they lived the rest of their lives.

Despite having started her schooling on such a bumpy path, Alexandra was very gifted in languages. She spoke German, French, and English fluently and was also quite comfortable with Italian. My father was her first and most accomplished student. She taught him French well enough that it became our primary language for the first few years of my life.

Her scoliosis did not slow down her social life. After the war, she enthusiastically joined the young people of Paris who spent their nights dancing through the nightclub circuit. She had a different dance partner for every type of dance. When I was young, my parents would host the biggest New Year's Eve bashes in their social circle. They would roll up the carpets and dance all night.

But what I remember were my mother's more sedentary activities: Scrabble, solitaire games, knitting and crocheting. Though the rest of our family pursued many sports, her back pain limited her activities. The only "exercise" she enjoyed was birding, and my parents traveled the world, chasing the best birding spots. That finally ended when airlines prohibited smoking on planes. My mother became so angry that, in protest, she boycotted flying.

Alexandra taught French to children, developing her own local program, FLES (French Language for Elementary School Children). When she was no longer funded for this innovative program, she became a French lecturer at Cornell.

There were very few indicators as I grew up that my mother had suffered traumas as a child. She was very self-conscious about her scoliosis and would point out that her condition had become so severe because of the malnutrition she had suffered during the war. I remember times when my mother's food memories would surface. There were certain foods that she refused to eat because they were associated with the hardships of eating the same thing day after day. She never ate chickpeas, Jerusalem artichokes, or rutabagas, and as a result, I was never introduced to these delicious foods until I was an adult.

I'm not sure if there is a connection to her years of hunger, but if there were leftovers, she would try to foist them on us, even when we made it abundantly clear that we were full.

She would plead, "Please finish this little piece so that it will be good weather tomorrow." Her insistence that all food was to be consumed far exceeded the normal "Jewish mama" guilt trip.

Underneath her happy, confident, and outspoken persona there lurked constant anxiety. Though Alexandra always kept a a reserve of Valium, I never remember her actually using it. She relied instead on her cigarettes to settle her overactive nerves. She took her first puff at age 14 and was hooked for life. We would plead with her to quit, knowing she was compromising her health and shortening her life.

Her reply to our pleas was "So I'll be dead a little longer." She died of cancer at age 78.

"Many people who read this will think, 'What an unlucky life.' But for me, it was lucky. It started well and ended well."

Curt and Hans, Fritz's two brothers

Fritz's two brothers, who were both arrested during Kristallnacht, survived the war. Curt, the eldest brother, and his wife, Lily, lived in Switzerland during the war and returned to Germany, where Curt resumed his career as a notary.

Hans owned the Kroch Bank, and for this reason the Nazis needed his expertise in order to keep the bank solvent. To prevent Hans from escaping, they arrested his wife, Ella, and kept her hostage in a concentration camp, promising that his wife would be kept alive as long as he continued to work for the bank. They did not keep their promise. Ella was murdered in Ravensbruck in 1942.

Hans and his children were able to escape. After the war, Hans moved to Jerusalem. There, as a memorial to his son Jacob, who died in the Israeli War of Independence, Hans built the Holy Land Hotel. On the beautiful grounds of the hotel, he constructed a 1:50 scale model of Jerusalem from the Second Temple time of King Herod, who built the temple in 37 B.C. The model is now on display at the Israel Museum.

Ella, wife of Hans, 1938

Hans Kroch

The Holy Land Hotel

Grete Frishman, Fritz's sister

Grete and her husband and son escaped Germany in 1933 to relocate in Belgium. They were communists and Jews, which was a deadly combination for German citizens. In Belgium, they were well situated to help orchestrate the smuggling operation for the three Kroch girls.

When Fritz Kroch came to Belgium to retrieve his daughters in early 1939, Grete and Marcel had been denied their visas to remain in Belgium and were abruptly sent back to Berlin. They applied for visas to Australia, which were immediately granted as a result of their connections with the famous General Sir John Monasch, a great hero during World War I. Grete and Fritz's sister Emmy had married Berthold Loebel Monasch, who was the first cousin of Sir John. They traveled to Toulon, France, and at the border between Germany and France, the train was stopped by a very drunk top SS commander who mistook Marcel for an old school friend and invited him for more drinks, leaving Grete and their son, Martin, waiting on the train, fearing that this was the end. Fortunately, Marcel was a very good clown, and for one hour he pretended to be this Nazi's old friend, laughing and drinking together. He returned no worse for the experience. The train was allowed to continue, and Toulon was reached, where they managed to take the last boat going to Australia, the HMS Ormonde.

In early 1952, Marcel and Grete joined Martin in London, where they lived in a center for Australian refugee artists in Hendon. Grete was an accomplished artist of oil paintings and etchings. Alexandra always felt a close bond with Grete, who died in 1972.

Grete top. Below, husband Marcel, and son Martin

Reunions in Mézières-en-Brenne
2015 and 2017

Many of the children of Peter, Alexandra, Judith, and Eva ("the cousins") have continued to visit each other regularly over the years. Our families have homes in Hong Kong, Germany, Italy, England, and the United States. Most live in Israel. We decided, one day as we were rejoicing in each other's company at our cousin Bettina and her husband, Rami's, winery near the Lebanon border, that we wanted to have our next cousins' reunion in France. More specifically, we wanted to visit Mézières-en-Brenne, the village that had hidden and sustained our parents. We contacted the mayor of Mézières, Jean-Louis Camus. He very graciously managed the details of our visit, which included a town hall meeting to which he invited the elder members of the village who remembered the Kroch family. He also invited descendants of Henri and Thérèse Morissé. Six Kroch cousins rented a beautiful inn an hour away in the Dordogne region of France. We arrived in Mézières-en-Brenne on a hot July morning for our rendezvous with the mayor.

Our first stop was at Les Troènes, the last house where the seven members of the Kroch family lived before they went into hiding. There we met Patrick and Jacki Morissé, the decendants of Henri and Thérèse Morissé. We were strangers gathering to commemorate an event that had brought together two unrelated families and bound them tightly. Seventy-five years ago the two families, different from each other in every way, had found themselves facing a common enemy. One family had lost every material procession and was fleeing for its life, and the other family, with so little to offer, had provided them with complete protection. The Kroch family had depended totally on the Morissé family to shelter them and save them from certain death.

The Kroch cousins had grown up hearing stories of the 2 x 2 meter shed that had hidden our family for three weeks, and ultimately had saved them from capture when other Jews from surrounding villages had been arrested. We had all tried to imagine seven people – and not just any people, but our people, our parents – living silently and fearfully in a space smaller than most of our bathrooms. We had each formed a picture of the hut and were hoping that it still existed.

Patrick and Jacki knew the location of the ruins of the hut. They explained that only the foundation remained and proceeded to take us on a rather complicated route into a fenced-in, grassy farmland lot adjoining woods filled with prickly briars. We followed them into the woods, picking our way through the thorny bushes that barred our passage and scratched our legs. They pointed out a pile of foundation stones, the only remnants of the three weeks spent living in the tiny tool shed. The pile of rubble and soil, arranged roughly in a square, did provide us with an idea of how small it was, and how incredible it was that seven people had evaded capture by spending their days in total silence, crammed into that tiny space. As I visualized the structure as it had been, I was overwhelmed with the magnitude of this moment. Here it was at last, the hiding place that had saved them. How small, how primitive.

We later gathered at the town hall, where we met the deputy mayor. She had organized a formal gathering that included elders from the village who remembered our family. We were surprised to hear that the Kroch family had not been the only Jewish family helped by this village. During the war, this information had to be kept secret. It wasn't until after the dangers were over that the citizens of Mézières realized that there were several villagers hiding Jews. The mayor and the police were also part of the resistance to stand up to the Nazis. Each citizen helped privately so as not to take a risk that Nazi collaborators discover their role as resisters.

This tradition of sheltering refugees continues to this day in Mézières. The ninety-year-old grande dame of the village explained that they had recently welcomed a Syrian refugee family to their community. This tiny French village considers it their mission to help others.

At one point during the town hall gathering, I addressed the Morissé family, "Your family worked hard all day, and then at night made dinner and fed our family. Henri and Thérèse Morissé hid our family and saved their lives even though it put their entire family at risk. And because of them, there are forty-six lives that wouldn't have been born." My cousin Bettina translated into French. This simple declaration embraced the core purpose of our reunion. How does one comprehend why a family makes a sacrifice of this magnitude? It needed to be acknowledged. Our parents survived because of this courageous family.

In Israel, there is an award that is given to non-Jewish individuals who saved the lives of Jews during World War II. The award is called "Righteous Among the Nations" or, as more commonly known, the Yad Vashem award, and is bestowed upon rescuers to: "Convey the gratitude of the State of Israel and the Jewish people to non-Jews who risked their lives to save Jews during the Holocaust. ... In 1963 the Remembrance Authority embarked upon a worldwide project to grant the title of Righteous Among the Nations to the few who helped Jews in the darkest time in their history." [24]

As of January 1, 2019 the State of Israel had bestowed 27,362 awards, many posthumously. Of those, 4,099 have been presented to French citizens.

The Yad Vashem website explains:

"More often than not the rescuers came from completely different backgrounds and had very little in common with the Jews for whom they risked their lives. Despite these differences and the stressful circumstances of helping Jews clandestinely, the ties between rescuers and the people they saved often developed into profoundly close relationships. The stressful circumstances of living clandestinely created strong bonds between the Righteous Among the Nations and the persons they saved. The memory of rescue – the noblest expression of sacrifice and solidarity as well as the terrible suffering it often entailed – continues to affect the families of both rescuers and rescued." [25]

When the Kroch cousins came face to face with the family of our rescuers, we were overwhelmed with gratitude and awe. The residents of Mézières-en-Brenne were also very moved that we had made this voyage to meet and to thank them. Following our visit, the spouse of one of my cousins, Yoram Zellner, put forward an application to bestow the Morissé family with the Yad Vashem award, which was eventually granted.

On June 23rd, 2017 several of the Kroch family cousins and two of Felix Goldschmidt's grandsons returned to Mézières-en-Brenne in order to attend the ceremonial presentation of the Yad Vashem award

*to the descendants of Henri and Thérèse Morissé. At that time there was
also the dedication of the Liberty Fountain that had been commissioned
by the village with money donated by the Kroch cousins. This monetary
gift was intended to offer special thanks and to honor the citizens of
the village who had provided sanctuary to the Kroch and Goldschmidt
families. Mayor Morève and the local police had protected the two
Jewish families and had warned the Kroch family of their impending
arrest in order to give them time to take cover, thereby saving their
lives.*

*This is a section of the speech given by Francois Guggenheim,
the vice president of the French Yad Vashem committee, which captures
the essence of this historic and moving ceremony. After first addressing
all the people individually who attended this occasion, he went on to say:*

"Dear friends,

It is in the name of the French Committee for Yad Vashem, of which I
have the honor to be the Vice-President, that I thank you, Mr. Mayor,
as well as all your team that I wish to greet now, to have organized this
ceremony, which is so symbolic and which will, undoubtedly, mark the
memory of everyone.

As most of you, I have the luck to be born after the war, and thus,
whatever we can do, whatever we can say:

- We can't understand what happened,
- We can't imagine the atrocities committed during that period,
- We can't express what the ones who survived to this period felt, day after day, even less the ones who died,
- We can't explain the inexplicable,
- We can't tolerate the unbearable,
- We can't ignore these millions of victims from the Holocaust, of the Shoah,
- We can't forget these vile coworkers of the Nazis, as a great number of our compatriots were, up to the highest state positions,

- We can't remain silent in front of our children; our duty is to pass on what our parents and grandparents have known, the big shame of the twentieth century, the shame of the country of human rights, the human shame which, until then, nobody could ever have imagined.

But this period so dark of our country, and of our European continent, also revealed the behavior of exceptional human beings who, at the risk of their lives, managed to show the whole humanity, that Man, if he wants, can always say 'NO' and refuse the unacceptable."

And so it was that in an unusual and moving twist to the normal Yad Vashem award that goes to an individual or family, this event also commemorated an entire village.

The Kroch family cousins (children of Peter, Eva, Judith, and Alexandra) had months earlier presented the Mézières-en-Brenne townspeople a monetary gift of appreciation to use as they pleased. They chose to erect this "Fountain of Liberty" memorial in the town center square.

Les Troènes - the house that the Kroch family rented after moving out of Les Vignes

The Goldschmidt's house in Mézières, Les Vignes. Note outside stairway, where many old and contemporary photographs were taken.

2015: Visiting Les Vignes, the home of the Goldschmidts during WWII. On the stairway from top to bottom: Amatsia and Michal (Judith), Celia (Alexandra), Eri (Peter), Bettina (Eva), Ben (Alexandra), and Ayala (Peter)

2017: Visiting Les Vignes again for the presentation of the Yad Vashem award. From top to bottom: Amatsia, Michal, Celia, Elie Goldschmidt (grandson of Félix and son of Jules), Ben, and Daniel Goldschmidt (grandson of Félix and son of René-Chmouel)

Madame Denise Morissé receiving the Righteous Among the Nations Award on behalf of her deceased parents in law: Henri and Thérèse Morissé. Also on the podium are Michal Kashti, daughter of Judith, Ido Bromber, Attaché to the Israel Ambassador, Daniel Goldschmidt, grandson of Félix Goldschmidt, Mayor Jean Louis Camus, and François Guguenheim, Vice-President of the French Yad Vashem committee

*Henri and Thérèse Morissé
on their wedding day*

*Descendants of Henri and Thérèse Morissé. The little girl (great, great
granddaughter of Thérèse and Henri) is holding a photograph of the wall that
stands in the Garden of the Righeous Among the Nations at the Yad Vashem
Museum in Jerusalem. That section of the wall has the engraved names of
Henri and Thérèse Morissé.*

IN MEMORY

Had any precarious step of their escape taken a different turn, the Kroch family would have been killed, and I would not have been born. From Peter, Eva, Judith, and Alexandra came 48 children, grandchildren, and great grandchildren, with more on the way.

The stories of Eva, Judith, and Alexandra and other fortunate survivors keep alive the memory of the six million Jews who were just like my mother and her family, but did not survive. We mourn all their descendants who were never born, and all of the non-Jews who were also murdered: the mentally and physically disabled, the Romas, those with different sexual orientations, and many others who were considered undesirable by the Nazis. We must honor all those who sacrificed their lives for the survival of the Jews; including soldiers, resistance fighters, and the non-Jewish citizens of Europe who helped to rescue those in peril.

To put this number "six million" into perspective, consider that 8.4 million people live in New York City. Los Angeles is the next largest city in the United States, with a population of almost four million. It is unfathomable to consider that the equivalent of an entire large city of innocent children, women and men were systematically tortured and murdered.

Future generations of Holocaust survivors have an obligation to hold, and to share the legacies of our ancestors. The Holocaust must never be forgotten, and never be repeated. Let us honor and be inspired by those who stood up against hate.

"Thou shalt not be a victim, thou shalt not be a perpetrator, but, above all, thou shalt not be a bystander."

— Yehuda Bauer

ENDNOTES

[1] *Nazi Germany 1933-1939: Early Stages of Persecution: How Hitler laid the groundwork for genocide*, My Jewish Learning, www.myjewishlearning.com.

[2] *Kristallnacht, A Nationwide Pogrom*, Holocaust Encyclopedia, United States Holocaust Memorial Museum, www.ushmm.org.

[3] *Boycott of Jewish Businesses,* Holocaust Encyclopedia, United States Holocaust Memorial Museum, www.ushmm.org.

[4] Also known as "The Jewish Question"

[5] *Indoctrination of Youth*, Holocaust Encyclopedia, United States Holocaust Memorial Museum, www.ushmm.org.

[6] Susan Zuccotti, *The Holocaust, the French, and the Jews,* 1993, 31.

[7] Zuccotti, 43.

[8] Ibid, 38.

[9] Ibid, 55-57.

[10] Ibid, 33.

[11] Ibid, 67.

[12] Ibid, 67-68.

[13] Ibid, 36-37.

[14] Ibid, 98-102.

[15] *The Vélodrome D'Hiver (Vél D'Hiv) Roundup*, Holocaust Encyclopedia, United States Holocaust Memorial Museum, www.ushmm.org.

[16] Zuccotti, 206-207.

[17] Zuccotti, 196.

[18] National Memorial of Montluc Prison, www.memorial-montluc.fr.

[19] *Klaus Barbie: The Butcher of Lyon*, Holocaust Encyclopedia, United States Holocaust Memorial Museum, www.ushmm.org.

[20] The sisters could not remember the name of the prison, so it was not possible to determine in which Lyon prison the Kroch family was incarcerated.

[21] *"Final Report of the Independent Commission of Experts Switzerland – Second World War,"* 114.

[22] *Refugees*, Holocaust Encyclopedia, United States Holocaust Memorial Museum, www.ushmm.org.

[23] Félix Goldschmidt's letters to his family, with permission from his family who have translated these letters from French into Hebrew and English:

Drancy, November 19, 1943

Dear Marguerite and dear children,

It's Friday today; departure is scheduled for tomorrow morning. They speak of Upper Silesia as our final destination. In all cases, we have provisions for 5 days of travel. Our stay in Drancy was not horrible, I made good friends there and, above all, I was able to benefit from relative freedom, within the limits imposed by the barbed wire. According to the news that we have received from there (Upper Silesia), the previous deportees enjoy it and are well fed. In any case, as I have already written, it is almost certain that my itinerary will change. In this case, as a precaution, you will not hear from me for a while. Don't worry about it; on the contrary – rest assured of my silence. The whole camp and the convoy are administered by ourselves, under the close supervision of these gentlemen; I was appointed as the leader of our wagon.

I am very happy to have received no package, I already have enough things to wear, enough underwear. I restocked my pharmacy; here all services are free (hairdresser, laundry, shoemaker, tailor, showers, etc.). My shoes have been re-sewn. With my blanket and another that I "borrowed" from L., I created a double sleeping bag, lined with wool that I removed from the mattresses. I also made mittens, socks and underpants, also from blankets, a pair of blue work pants, 3 sweaters, 1 muff, etc. Our "snacks" for 5 days of travel: a 2kg loaf of bread, 500g of meat, chocolate, cheese, etc., in a satchel. I will definitely not eat everything! (You can see all the work that our kitchen team does, in order to prepare everything. We are 1200 "travelers," the kind I saw in Gurs). For this evening, we are staying in rooms of 50, one room per wagon. My room is the best and is known throughout the camp, we are all in a fairly cheerful mood, the "travelers" from the other rooms come to visit us; they say it encourages them. The tailor of Ch. Is in my room, and consequently in my wagon; so, he must "follow" me, is in my room, and therefore in my wagon.

I asked a painter in my room to paint our motto "Proud and worthy" on the white walls. You cannot imagine how immensely proud I am to live these great minutes, which galvanize me and fill me, to the very depths of my being, with a feeling of gratitude, of absolute happiness, although, or because that, I am constantly thinking of you. But – and you will understand me, because you know me and you know why I am here and why I am proud of it – I almost regret that you cannot share my joy and my amazing calm. It is here that I finally feel pure pride in being Jewish, on the front lines facing the last charge of the Barbarians. In addition, I am not alone, and many of our brothers and sisters have finally understood and become Jews here again. Léopold Metzger, my cousin, the head of the neighboring wagon, thinks the same way as I do and acts on his comrades, with the same success. We have had long conversations together, and some issues and ideas have taken on new meaning for us here. To be Jewish is above all to be human.

I have a lot to do: providing social services and food in preparation for the departure of my 49 (companions) keeps me busy day and night, as well as other important preparations for "departure."

It is not yet cold and the rooms are heated (central heating) and, in the fireplaces, we make coffee, tea etc. Even if we arrive in Upper Silesia, everyone will work according to their talents, but you can be sure that I will find work on the way as well, which will not displease me at all!

This evening there will be a religious service in the part of the camp reserved for the deportees. Rabbi Schönberg, who is himself a deportee, will speak, and that will surely be very pleasant.

They just gave me a messenger bag and a woolen hood.

I have no regrets and I don't want you to have, either. We have always agreed on everything and we must continue the same today. I would be delighted to know that you truly and joyfully share my tranquility and my certain confidence in a near and happy future. None of us are sad here, and tomorrow, at the station, we will sing, for us and for them, the Hatikvah and the Marseillaise.

The sun sets. I embrace you all ardently and send you my happy blessings; as I have always done and as I will do again soon, I admire you, I look, with my eyes wide open and smiling, in your beloved eyes. My eyes are wide open and I smile.

You will soon be happy again with your Félix and your Papa.

~~~~~~~~~~~~~

Drancy, November 19, 1943

Dear Marguerite and dear children,

When you receive this letter, you will probably have certain reasons to believe that I have disappeared; that my fugue did not succeed (that of tomorrow or another, as I promised myself that I will do my utmost to find you) or that the climate in Upper

Silesia was not good for me.

However, and I insist on this, do not give up hope of seeing me again until the deportees have returned for several months.

Once this date has passed, however, do not continue to hold on to a vain hope, continue your life, as many people have done since the start of the war, without constantly turning around. I know that you will not forget me, as I will not have forgotten any of you. From time to time, say every November 20, maybe more often, but not every day – I ask you – you can devote a few minutes to the memory of the one who loved you until his last minute (I ask forgiveness for this solemn and dismal tone, which I hate; I am not used to writing this kind of letter). But apart from these rare moments, which I accept because they correspond to the magnificent years that we lived together, I don't want my memory to overwhelm you to the point of clouding your life. I know that Life overcomes all mourning, but I want you to know that I have always loved and aspired to happiness, and that I want to know that you are happy. When you think of me, remember, without bitterness, the wonderful – and despite everything long – journey that we lived together, hand in hand, across roads that were not always trivial, almost always smiling. Remember, Marguerite, the beauty of our first meetings – we were only children – and of all the happy occasions and the short but revitalizing sorrows – and you, my children, remember our warm camaraderie – because Mom and I were real comrades, for each other and for you, too. We were not a family but an enthusiastic team. Stay a team and if you think of your old comrade, think of me with a smile on your lips. Do not blame yourself for feeling happiness in your life again: it is I who beg you to be happy, as I always wanted you to be and as I always have been.

We will never know the true meaning of life. ... Our existence on Earth is too heavily subject to laws too mysterious for our modest understanding. Our mind will never be able to understand everything and say, this is the Truth. Science cannot explain everything, as for Faith, it is not intended to explain everything, either. We just have faith, and it lifts us up. But Faith cannot be commanded. Between these two poles, the mind is free, and only Consciousness – because Consciousness exists; we know it – must be your compass. What you do in good conscience, having done it thinking it was the Truth, will always be right. I do not leave you guidelines; I myself am still looking for my own way. Each must be their own guide, unless he finds higher spirits who can point him in the right direction. But don't look too much outside of yourself.

You, my children, if you hesitate, confide in Mom. She is authentic, sincere and good. Follow its path until you are sure you have found your own direction, within your consciousness.

If you love me (you love me; I know it), remember that each of you is part of me. Therefore, love one another, always stay united. Do what is Good and remember that the greatest joy is to be found in the feeling of Done. Do not insist on life at all costs: these few years on Earth are not so important; it is better to live little by fighting, than to make one's existence last for long years of moral and intellectual mediocrity.

Love is also an exceptional thing. Later, each of you will love your life partner, just as Mom and I loved each other. You will also love your Brothers and all of Humanity, as I myself loved them. Don't be small. The Great is the most beautiful.

Don't think of avenging me personally. They hurt us a lot, but the battle between them and me was fierce. I attacked them, they defended themselves, but I won my war, because I made several victims in their ranks – if all goes well, I will continue to do the same tomorrow and the days to come – and they will have killed only me. Do not confuse Justice and Vengeance. Justice is a Duty, but Vengeance is a passion. I would not want my life, and especially not that of my sons, to be obsessed with the desire for revenge. Be builders, rather than avengers.

My writing becomes weak; I added water to the ink to keep our conversation going.

I kiss you all and hug you tightly. I kiss you, Marguerite, and I say thank you for all that you have brought me and for what you have given to our children. To you, my children, my most ardent blessings.

We may see each other again – hopefully – up there.

Your Félix
Your Dad
~~~~~~~~~~~~

Letter sent from the train deporting him to Auschwitz:

Dear Marguerite.

Try to locate, in Drancy's office, the "le guet" I left (referring to a legal document allowing her remarriage in the event of his disapperance). I hope that you can use it and start a new wonderful life, with the man who will make you happy and whose hand I shake with sincere affection. I hope he will be calmer than me, but that he will be as well intentioned as I am.

Kissing, Félix

[24] *The Righteous Among the Nations*, Yad Vashem, www.yadvashem.org.

[25] *Our Jewish Family: The Bond Between Rescuer and Rescued, The Righteous Among the Nations,* Yad Vashem, www.yadvashem.org.

Discussion Questions

1. Trust is a major theme running through this story. Which events depict how the Kroch family is forced to trust strangers? Have you ever been in a situation where you must trust someone that you don't know in order to help you navigate a difficult predicament? How is this situation different or similar to the Kroch family situation?

2. Food accessibility and hunger is a constant focus of the sisters. What are some examples of this? Describe some of the ways the Kroch family's relationship to food and nourishment change over the course of the story. Has there ever been a time in your life when food accessibility changed? If so, how has that experience influenced you later in life?

3. Each sister copes with the hardships and fears differently. How much do you think is due to their age and birth order and how much is due to her personality? How do you cope when you are placed in very difficult situations? Which person's coping style is most similar to your own?

4. Throughout the story, the girls refer to their optimism. What factors enable the family to keep such a positive outlook on such a grim situation?

5. Who is your favorite character, the person you can most relate to? Why?

6. What is bravery? Who in this story most embodies bravery?

7. Several characters in this story risk their lives to save the lives of others. Who are they? What do you think propels some people to be rescuers who risk their lives in the process? Are they profoundly different than you or anyone you know? What do you think you would have done in the same situation?

8. The Holocaust is not an isolated event in history. What genocides are happening right now around the world?

9. Do you think the fact that the Kroch family started out with so much wealth made it easier or more difficult for them to cope with their diminishing standard of living? Why?

10. Jews lost all their rights and became the targets of racism. How does this compare to people of color in the US? Can you identify situations happening right now in this country where this is happening?

11. The Kroch family survived because of luck, careful planning, and the help of others. Millions of Jews and other victims of WW2 were not so fortunate. There were many who planned carefully and received help from others who still didn't survive because their luck ran out. Those who did survive often feel/ felt guilty. Why do you think they felt this way? Were their feelings justified?

12. Is there someone in your family that you would like to interview? What is it that you would like to capture about their life story? Are there obstacles that prevent you from doing this? Do you think they would enjoy being interviewed?

BIBLIOGRAPHY

Bhatia, Rukmani. *From Israelite to Jew: Anti-Semitism in Vichy France & Its Impact on French-Jewish Identity After WWII.* Wellesley College Digital Scholarship and Archive, Honors Thesis Collection, 2012.

Brustein, Willam I. and King, Ryan D. "Anti-Semitism in Europe Before the Holocaust," *International Political Science Review*, 2004, Vol 25, No. 1, 35–53.

Final Report of the Independent Commission of Experts Switzerland – Second World War. Zürich: Pendo Verlag GmbH, 2002.

Gilbert, Martin. *The Holocaust: A History of the Jews in Europe During the Second World War.* New York: Holt, Rienehart, and Winston, 1985.

Independent Commission of Experts Switzerland. *Second World War: Switzerland and Refugees in the Nazi Era.* Bern, Switzerland, 1999. (ISBN 3-908661-07-2. English version has been translated from German and French original texts.)

Kashti-Kroch, Judith. *Running for Survival: The story of a young girl's flight from the Nazis 1938-42.* London: Janus Publishing Company, 1993.

Koonz, Claudia. *Mothers in the Fatherland: Women, the Family, and Nazi Politics.* New York: St. Martin's Press, 1987.

Larson, Erik. *In the Garden of Beasts: Love, Terror, and an American Family in Hitler's Berlin.* US: Broadway Books, 2012.

Vered, Yael. *Là où il n'y a pas d'hommes tâche d'être un homme...* , (Translated from Hebrew to French by Jules Goldschmidt, 2006) Israel: Félix Rav Ha'Aliloth, 1999 and Paris: Parole et Silence, 2006.

Zuccotti, Susan. *The Holocaust, The French, and The Jews.* US: Harper Collins Publishers, 1993.

Rescuers, The Righteous, and Resistance

Block, Gay and Drucker, Malka. *Rescuers: Portraits of Moral Courage in the Holocaust.* US: Holmes and Meier Publishers, Inc., 1992.

Fogelman, Eva. *Conscience and Courage: Rescuers of Jews During the Holocaust.* New York: Anchor Books, 1994.

Gilbert, Martin. *The Righteous: The Unsung Heroes of the Holocaust.* New York: Henry Holt and Company, 2003.

Hallie, Philip. *Lest Innocent Blood Be Shed: The Story of the Village of Le Chambon and How Goodness Happened Here.* New York: HarperCollins Publishers, 1979 & 1994.

Klempner, Mark. *The Heart Has Reasons: Dutch Rescuers of Jewish Children during the Holocaust,* 2006 & 2012.

Moorehead, Caroline. *A Train in Winter. An Extraordinary Story of Women, Friendship, and Resistance in Occupied France.* New York: HarperCollins Publishers, 2012.

Paldiel, Mordecai. *The Righteous Among the Nations: Rescuers of Jews During the Holocaust.* Jerusalem: The Jerusalem Publishing House Ltd. and Yad Vashem, 2007.

Purnell, Sonia. *A Woman of No Importance: The Untold Story of the American Spy Who Helped Win World War II.* Penguin Books, April 2019.

Online Resources

Antisemitism from the Enlightenment to World War I. Facing History and Ourselves: www.facinghistory.org.

Boycott of Jewish Business. Holocaust Encyclopedia, United States Holocaust Memorial Museum: www.ushmm.org.

Félix Goldschmidt. Holocaust Encyclopedia, United States Holocaust Memorial Museum: www.ushmm.org.

Ferrero, Shaul. *Switzerland and the Refugees Fleeing Nazism: Documents on the German Jews Turned Back at the Basel Border in 1938-1939.* (Translated from French by Ruth Morris), Vol. XXVII, pp. 203-234, Jerusalem: Yad Vashem Studies, 1999, Yad Vashem: The World Holocaust Rememberance Center: www.yadvashem.org.

Gurs. holocaustmusic.ort.org.

Holocaust badges. Holocaust Memorial Center, www.holocaustcenter.org.

Indoctrination of Youth. Holocaust Encyclopedia, United States Holocaust Memorial Museum, www.ushmm.org.

Introduction to the Holocaust. Holocaust Encyclopedia, United States Holocaust Memorial Museum: www.ushmm.org.

Jews in Pre-War Germany. Holocaust Encyclopedia, United States Holocaust Memorial Museum: www.ushmm.org.

Jewish Life in Europe Before the Holocaust. Holocaust Encyclopedia, United States Holocaust Memorial Museum: www.ushmm.org.

Klaus Barbie. Holocaust Encyclopedia, United States Holocaust Memorial Museum: encyclopedia.ushmm.org.

Kristallnacht, A Nationwide Pogrom. Holocaust Encyclopedia, United States Holocaust Memorial Museum: www.ushmm.org.

Maginot Line. Wikipedia: en.wikipedia.org.

Maginot Line. Holocaust Encyclopedia, United States Holocaust Memorial Museum: www.ushmm.org.

Music, Memory, and Resistance during Holocaust. Facing History and Ourselves: www.facinghistory.

Montluc Prison. Educational Program, National Memorial of Montluc Prison. www.memorial-montluc.fr.

Nazi Germany 1933-1939. Early Stages of Persecution: How Hitler laid the groundwork for genocide. My Jewish Learning: www.myjewishlearning.com.

Refugees. Holocaust Encyclopedia, United States Holocaust Memorial Museum: www.ushmm.org.

Righteous Among the Nations. Yad Vashem: The World Holocaust Rememberance Center: www.yadvashem.org.

The Vélodrome D'Hiver (Vél D'Hiv) Roundup. Holocaust Encyclopedia, United States Holocaust Memorial Museum: www.ushmm.org.

Willingham II, Robert Allen, PhD and Crew, David, Supervisor. *Jews in Leipzig, Nationality and Community in the 20th Century,* The University of Texas at Austin, 2005: repositories.lib.utexas.edu.

Books by and about the Second Generation of Holocaust Survivors

Epstein, Helen, *Children of the Holocaust: Conversations with Sons and Daughters of Survivors.* New York: Putnam and New York: Penguin, 1979 & 1988.

Rasia Kliot, and Mitsios, Helen. *Waltzing with the Enemy: A Mother and Daughter Confront the Aftermath of the Holocaust.* New York: Lambda Publishers, Inc., 2011.

Rosensaft, Menachem Z. Ed. *God, Faith and Identity from the Ashes: Reflections of Children and Grandchildren of Holocaust Survivors*. Vermont: Jewish Lights Publishing, 2015.

Wardi, Dina. *Memorial Candles, Children of the Holocaust.* Israel: Maxwell-Macmillan-Keter, (Hebrew) 1990, London, US and Canada: Routledge, (English translator Naomi Goldblum) 1992.

ACKNOWLEDGEMENTS

First and foremost, I would like to thank Eva, Judith, and Alexandra who did what was so difficult for survivors of the Holocaust, and that was to dredge up traumatic memories. We, the descendants of the three sisters, are fortunate to have our mothers' memories preserved forever. Many of my fellow second generation survivors of the Holocaust experience deep regret and sadness not to have heard the stories of their survivor parents, who refused to talk about it. Quite understandably, for those survivors, the only way they could cope was to leave those traumas behind and move forward.

Eva and Judith most graciously agreed to allow me to include their testimonials in this book. Without their contributions, there would be no book. They spent many hours in 2016 meeting with me to help fill in missing pieces. I wish they were alive to read it.

A most important contributor to this book was my niece Ariana Littauer. Had she not taken on the laborious task of transcribing hours of audio recording, I never would have had Alexandra's transcripts, which were the starting point and inspiration to write this book. She also continued the interviews with her grandmother in order to fill in missing pieces.

Many other people contributed in some way to make this all happen. Early on, the encouragement and support of accomplished authors gave me the confidence to stick with it. Andrew Solomon, one of the most highly acclaimed non-fiction writers of our generation, offered a very flattering endorsement. Ellen Schmidt, an award winning poet and writing coach was very complimentary, urging me to publish. The support of these two writers boosted my confidence tremendously.

I am so grateful to my cousin Michal Zellner who hosted me and facilitated my interviews with her mother Judith and our aunt Eva during my visit to Israel during the summer of 2016.

I also could not have written this book without the help of my cousin Bettina, daughter of Eva. Bettina knew that her mother had dictated her memoirs; however, Eva had specifically instructed Bettina not to share them until after her death. I asked Bettina to inquire whether her mother would permit me to use her memoirs in my book, and Eva immediately agreed. Bettina then searched for and found the memoirs including a version that had been translated into English. She made copies of the several hundred pages of documents and sent them to me by snail mail from Israel.

Many of my relatives and the descendants of the rescuers scoured through family albums to find the perfect photos. I thank my cousins Ayala Havron, Bettina Na'aman, Michal Zellner, and Amatsia Kashti.

My brother Ben has been my "go-to" person, helping me to track down photos or to check up on a family fact. His phenomenal memory has come to my rescue on many occasions.

Special thanks also to Marie-Hélène Foufounis, the granddaughter of Marceau Boucheny, and to Elie and Daniel Goldschmidt, the grandsons of Félix Goldschmidt. My thanks as well to Liliane Bidault, retired Deputy Mayor of Mézières-en-Brenne who sent photographs of Mr. and Mrs. Morissé.

I am indebted to Emmanuelle Burstein, my close friend from France who helped me with research. Her perfect English was very useful when I needed French translations.

My wonderful copy editor and graphic designer worked tirelessly with me on placement of photos, the design of the map and the family, and the overall production and layout of the book. Without the tremendous help of Katrina Morse, this book would have never been published.

And last, but not least, I thank my husband Dan for his unwavering support. In his quiet, loving way he would gently remind me that I needed to take a break after spending too much time on the computer. He also provided much helpful feedback after reading countless drafts.

Celia Clement received her BA from Cornell and her MSW from Columbia. Celia is a retired school social worker with a specialty in bullying prevention. She and her husband raised three children. She lives in upstate NY with her husband in an 1830s farmhouse.

Visit:
www.celia-clement.com
for more photos and educational resources.

Contact:
celia.threesisters@gmail.com

Made in the USA
Middletown, DE
06 August 2020